The **PHARMACIST'S GUIDE** *to*

CONQUERING STUDENT LOAN$

Your Financial Pharmacist presents . . .

The PHARMACIST'S GUIDE *to*
CONQUERING STUDENT LOAN$

HOW TO CONFIDENTLY CHOOSE THE BEST PAYOFF STRATEGY THAT **SAVES YOU THE MOST MONEY**

Tim Church, PharmD, CDE

Disclaimer: This publication is designed to provide accurate and authoritative information with regard to the subject matter covered. The information in the book is not intended to replace or conflict with the financial advice provided by your designated professional(s) and may not be suitable for your personal situation. The ultimate decision to make any changes regarding your finances should be determined only by you and or your designated financial professional(s). The author and Your Financial Pharmacist LLC disclaim all liability in connection with the use of this book.

Editors: Justin Greer and Rochelle Deans

ISBN-13: 979-8-62108-927-6

TABLE OF CONTENTS

FOREWORD

By Timothy Ulbrich

In 2009, I found myself newly married, completing residency training, and still riding the high of getting my Doctor of Pharmacy degree. All was good except for one very significant reality.

I had more than $200,000 of student loan debt staring me in the face.

"It isn't even stupid debt," I rationalized. No credit card debt. No fancy cars. No extravagant toys. My wife, Jess, and I seemed to be living a normal, reasonable, and responsible life.

I rationalized in my mind that there was no need to worry. After all, my classmates were dealing with the same problem. It just came with the territory. Nothing a six-figure income couldn't handle. It was all normal. Right?

Wrong.

After wandering without a plan for three years, in 2012, the humbling reality finally set in.

I was broke.

I had a great income, but didn't own anything and owed a whole lot.

At the time, despite Jess and I earning approximately $500,000 of income since graduating from school, we had a net worth (assets minus liabilities) of *negative $225,000.*

This humbling reality of having a negative net worth and spinning our wheels financially hit Jess and I over the head hard. We had come to realize that this reality of being broke meant that:

- Despite our hopes and dreams, we were not in a position to move to a larger home in a more convenient location.

- We were not able to go on the vacations we had desired or, if we did, we would feel stressed due to delaying progress on paying down the debt.

- We were not in a position to give to those in need at the level we had desired.

With reality sinking in, I found myself confused. Why in the world was I feeling like I was living paycheck to paycheck despite having a six-figure income?

I also felt trapped that in the event of an emergency or wanting to make a job change in the future, that decision was largely made for me since I had so much debt. Talk about being financially vulnerable.

You see, I have talked with thousands of pharmacists and students over the past several years and most have a desire to put a plan in place to pay off their student loans. It rarely is a question of desire. Rather, they get overwhelmed with the numerous options available and choosing what the "best" option may be considering their personal situation and other competing financial priorities.

The result is often inaction or sticking with the status quo despite there likely being a better path forward. Dreaming or talking about paying off your student loans and devising and executing a plan to do so are two very different things.

What I was missing during my own journey was a roadmap, a guide, a how-to that was customized for the pharmacy professional.

Tim Church has invested hundreds, if not thousands, of hours in understanding this topic and finding a way to succinctly teach this in a way that results in action. He has translated that work into *The Pharmacist's Guide to Conquering Student Loans*, the first comprehensive student loan repayment guide available specifically for pharmacists and student pharmacists.

In *The Pharmacist's Guide to Conquering Student Loans,* Tim walks you through, step by step, how to choose the student loan repayment option that is best for your personal situation. Whether you are a pharmacy student trying to learn more about the options available, a recent graduate in the midst of choosing a repayment strategy, a resident or fellow wondering how to handle loans during the training years, someone struggling with a financial hardship such as a job loss, *or* a seasoned practitioner wondering whether or not you have the best repayment strategy in place, this book is for you!

Before you flip the page and get started on this journey, I want you to reflect for a moment about how you feel when you think about your student loans.

Perhaps you feel anxious, fearful, annoyed, or uncertain as to whether the plan you have in place is the right one. That feeling is justified, considering the choosing the "right" or "wrong" repayment option can mean a difference of tens of thousands of dollars!

Imagine for a moment you have evaluated all your repayment options available, considered the pros/cons, determined the best option for your personal situation, and now have a repayment plan that is on autopilot?

How are you feeling now?

If you're ready to take control of your student loan debt rather than the other way around, flip the page and let's get started!

Onward to financial freedom!

Timothy R. Ulbrich, PharmD
Co-Founder & CEO
Your Financial Pharmacist

Introduction

THE UNFORTUNATE REALITY

I'll never forget the day my wife and I finally paid off our student loan debt.

In fact, we still have a screenshot of the $0 loan balance!

We were overjoyed, to say the least. We felt accomplished. We felt relieved.

Finally, we did it!

Andria and I had conquered the $400,000 of student loan debt that had plagued us right from the start of our marriage.

$400,000! Gone!

No more saying no to everything.

No more anxiety about doing the things we wanted to do while still funding our financial goals.

No more payments!

And my wife was ready to finally get a cat.

The deep sacrifices we made to limit our spending finally paid off and we were so ready to move on with our lives.

But once that highly anticipated moment had come and gone, feelings other than happiness and relief set in. Ones that I didn't necessarily expect or want.

I was angry and frustrated, and I had some major regrets!

Weird, right?

For you to understand why those feelings were popping up, I need to go back a bit.

For the first year and half of my career in my government position, I had no idea of how to best manage my money and especially didn't know what to do about my student loans.

Prior to graduation, during capstone, I recall being graced by a visit with a "financial advisor" who came to speak about financial planning. I was excited because I was completely in the dark about what I was going to do with the heap of student loans. I needed at least some general tips on how to be successful with tackling my debt.

Well, the two-hour session came and went and I honestly did not feel any better. The majority of time was spent talking about life and disability insurance.

Sound familiar?

No information was given about strategies for taking down student loans or what the best option would be for me. Plus, since I was in the first graduating class at a new pharmacy school, there weren't any alumni I could reach out to for some sound advice.

That essentially meant I would be relying on my own experience, as well as the opinions and influence of my parents, relatives, and friends, on how to best manage money and what to do about my $25,000 car loan and $200,000 student loan debt. (This was my portion of the overall debt prior to getting married.)

Let's just say my parents weren't the best with money. I was happy when my cousin gave me the gift of an audiobook from a popular personal finance personality. I needed something to pass the time for my road trip from Ohio to Florida where I was about to start my residency.

Within the first 30 minutes, I was hooked. From the humor and intensity of the author to the simple and practical advice he was dishing out, I thought: *This is it! This is what I have been looking for.*

Save money and get out of debt. The prescription he gave to everyone.

This advice isn't necessarily an earth-shattering revelation, but hearing stories of people doing extreme things like eating rice and beans or moving in with parents to become free from their debt was very inspirational.

It *seemed* to make perfect sense, so that's what I focused on. My objective and game plan were clear. Get rid of my car loan and student loans as fast as possible, and try not to have a mental breakdown while doing so.

And that's exactly what I did.

Eventually, I was free of debt.

But unlike the inspiring debt-free stories that depict people ecstatic in their victory, for me, it honestly felt bittersweet.

This was all because of *the way* I paid off my student loans.

It turns out that the cookie-cutter financial advice I had been religiously following in my early career turned out to be *the* biggest financial mistake of my life.

Working for the government meant I was eligible for some potential loan repayment and forgiveness programs. Unfortunately, tuition reimbursement was not available at the time I was hired, but I *was* automatically eligible for the Public Service Loan Forgiveness, or PSLF, program.

I didn't know much about it, but it seemed like a good option.

However, the idea of going this route came and went pretty quickly. My newfound personal finance guru put the kibosh on that by saying things on his podcast like "why would you want to be in debt for 10 years" and "are you really going to rely on the government to follow through?"

He certainly had some valid arguments and there's no doubt that those options are still controversial today. At the time, unfortunately, his arguments were enough to sway me from even considering options beyond *pay off debt as fast as possible.*

So there I was, debt-free after eight years of paying out around $250,000 for my $200,000 student loan debt, thanks to interest.

That's when those odd, negative feelings started to kick in.

3

By forgoing PSLF, I failed to understand the huge opportunity cost of my choice.

First, I could have paid significantly less money toward my student loans over 10 years. With my average salary, I estimate I would have paid somewhere around $130,000, and the rest would have been forgiven tax-free.

You're probably thinking as I did initially—that I had made a $120,000 mistake.

Unfortunately, it's even worse!

You see, the average monthly payments in my accelerated plan were around $3,000, which did not leave much for investing and retirement savings.

Assuming I would have been making my 120 income-driven payments through PSLF, I would have never paid more than about $1,300 per month.

But what if I would have maxed out my TSP (government 401k equivalent), assuming a net rate of return of 5% for 10 years, while paying off my loans through the program?

Here's how my situation would have looked different.

Instead of being debt-free in 8 years after paying $250,000 with about $100,000 in my retirement account, I could have been debt-free in 10 years, paid around $100,000 with $250,000 in my retirement account.

When I did this math for the first time, it stung.

Because payments through PSLF are based on your adjusted gross income, you actually get rewarded when you make traditional contributions to your 401k. They lower your taxable income, thereby lowering your student loan payments, all while you get to take advantage of interest.

If only I would have fully known my options from the start and what the implications of this decision would be.

Now, I wouldn't say my decisions put me in a *terrible* financial position, but it could have been so much better.

The point of sharing this story is that you're going to be faced with or are already facing pretty significant student loan debt and you can't afford to make any mistakes.

Despite what you may have heard from friends, family, the internet, or financial gurus, there is no one-size-fits-all plan that will work for every pharmacist when it comes to student loans, so you have to know your options.

The Unfortunate Reality

Pharmacy graduates now carry student loan debt that exceeds an average of $172,000, with interest rates typically hovering between 6 and 8%. That's even putting it lightly, considering those who graduate from private institutions have mortgage-sized loan balances of over $200,000!

In addition, many carry undergraduate debt that increases their total student loan balance. This leaves most starting their careers with an extremely negative net worth.

Unfortunately, it's not just that student loan balances have greatly risen over time. Pharmacists' salaries are not even close to keeping pace.

Until 2011, the annual median pharmacist salary was greater than the median student loan debt. Every year since then, the opposite has been true. Not only that, but the gap continues to widen.

Although pharmacy is not the only profession with this issue, the rate of salary growth has been lagging compared to the growth among all healthcare workers, as reported by Drug Channels.

Plus, you are likely going to be facing additional job market challenges that previous generations of pharmacists didn't have to deal with that will directly impact your ability to manage your debt.

For example, the Bureau of Labor Statistics reports the expected job outlook as 0% growth for 2018-2028, and many pharmacists already feel this by expressing difficulty in finding their first job in saturated markets or even being let go from their current employer because of the closure of many brick and mortar locations.

Beyond that, many pharmacists are having their hours cut from 40 hours to 32 hours per week or even lower, drastically reducing their salaries.

This is the unfortunate reality pharmacy graduates are now facing.

What to Expect from this Book

I know firsthand how overwhelming it can be dealing with massive amounts of student loan debt and the impact it can have on the many aspects of your life.

That's why I want to help you develop a plan.

The goal of this book is to equip you with the key information you need to know to understand your student loans inside and out and teach you the best strategies to eliminate them.

I'll kick off chapter 1 by getting organized with your student loan debt. In chapter 2, I'll go into an overview of all the student loan payoff strategies, followed by a discussion on forgiveness options in chapters 3 and 4.

In chapter 5, I'll talk about the strategies outside of forgiveness and what refinancing options look like. In chapter 6, I'll break down how to pick your best strategy. Finally, I'll conclude in chapters 7, 8, and 9 with how to manage competing financial goals, how to manage your loans as a fellow or resident, and what to do with your loans if you experience a job loss or financial hardship.

Although this book is geared for the new pharmacy graduate, it can be a great resource even if you've already started paying down your loans and need a fresh look at your strategy.

Overall, my goal is for you to feel confident that the plan you choose is one that not only saves you the most money in the long term but also aligns with your financial goals.

That way, you can feel absolutely awesome when you crush your loans without the feelings of regret I experienced.

Although this book is comprehensive, there's no way to address every scenario one has with their student loans, so your personal situation may require additional attention.

If that's you, then I would recommend reaching out to another Tim on our team. Tim Baker, our Certified Financial Planner™, offers detailed student loan analyses and a lot more.

You can go to www.yourfinancialpharmacist.com/planning for more information.

Now it's time to get started!

Chapter 1

GET ORGANIZED

Before jumping into student loan payoff strategies and developing an overall game plan, it's important to know exactly how much you owe and who you owe.

You may have no idea how much student loan debt you've racked up over the years and probably don't want to find out.

Right? I get it!

Looking your debt straight in the eye can be scary and overwhelming! I've been there. But trust me, you'll soon find clarity by seeing exactly what you're facing and creating an inventory of your federal and private loans. I'll walk you through the process step by step.

If you have already been paying on your loans, it doesn't hurt to inventory your loans again to make sure you have the most up-to-date records.

Here we go.

Inventory Your Federal Loans

Unless you used a private lender or refinanced your loans after pharmacy school, you likely have federal loans through the Department of Education.

You can access all your federal loan information through the National Student Loan Data System (NSLDS). This is the national record of all of your loans and grants during their complete life cycle. It contains information on your outstanding balance, outstanding interest, interest rate, and associated servicer. The NSLDS is updated at least every 30 days.

To access the NSLDS and inventory your federal student loans, follow these three easy steps:

1. Log in to your Federal Student Aid account at www.studentaid.gov

Log in using your FSA ID and password. If you don't have an FSA ID or can't remember your password, just follow the appropriate steps to create an ID or to reset your password.

2. Identify your total outstanding balance and weighted interest

Here it is, the moment you haven't been waiting for—the one you've probably been avoiding! Take a deep breath and remember that learning the details of what you owe will help you come up with a payment strategy. It's a critical step for you to start tackling this debt! Later on, I'll lay out all of the available repayment options so that you can determine the best payoff strategy.

Once you've logged in to your account, you'll see a loan balance and weighted interest amount listed. The weighted interest is the average interest between all of your federal loans. For example, if you have two loans, one with a $100,000 balance and a 4% interest rate and another with a $100,000 balance and a 6% interest rate, your total loan balance of $200,000 would have a weighted interest rate of 5%.

3. Identify individual outstanding loans, interest rates, and the servicer of those loans

On the same page that you see your total loan balance and weighted interest rate, you'll see a list of your individual loans and additional details about that loan, like the type of loan, loan balance, and interest rate.

The list could be as long as a CVS receipt.

There are a number of types of federal loans that you may see that are either subsidized or unsubsidized loans. When you click on the plus sign on the right side of an individual loan, you'll see even more information about it, like the date the loan originated, the servicer, and eligible repayment plans for that specific loan.

At this point, don't get too bogged down with all of the types of eligible repayment options, as this will be covered in detail in upcoming chapters. For right now, just focus on getting a complete list of all of your loans, including the balance, interest rate, and servicer.

If you feel that the loan information listed isn't accurate due to missing, duplicate, or incorrect information, first check the dates to confirm that the information listed is current. If you do notice an issue, contact the servicer to try to solve the discrepancies. If needed, you can file a formal complaint using the FSA feedback system or, as a final step in finding a solution, file a formal complaint to FSA Ombudsman.

Types of Federal Loans

The specific type of federal loans you have is important to know, as it has implications for how interest is accruing, eligibility for forgiveness programs, and deciding which loans to consolidate or refinance.

Although these names are confusing and just listening to them can cause unexpected somnolence, it is important to pay attention.

Federal loans are either subsidized or unsubsidized.

With subsidized loans, interest does not accrue while in school, during the grace period, or if you're in deferment. If you're not sure what these terms are, don't worry; I will cover them in more depth later.

Loans considered to be subsidized include Direct Subsidized (typically from undergraduate school), Direct Consolidation (from multiple subsidized loans), Perkins, and Subsidized FFEL, which stands for Federal Family Education Loan Program.

Unsubsidized loans will likely make up the bulk of the money you borrowed for your PharmD. They accrue interest the day they are disbursed and continue to accrue while you're in school, during the grace period, and while in deferment or forbearance.

Unfortunate, right?

This is the reason why, if you're checking your loan balance for the first time since you graduated, it looks a lot bigger than what you recall borrowing.

Unsubsidized loans include Direct Unsubsidized, Direct Plus, Direct Consolidation, and Unsubsidized FFEL.

Besides classifying loans based on whether interest is accruing, they are also broken down by which federal loan program they are in.

There are two federal loan programs in play when it comes to your federal student loans. The first is the William D. Ford Direct Student Loan Program, which is the largest federal student loan program, with the U.S. Department of Education serving as the lender.

The second is the Federal Perkins loan program, which is a need-based loan program for those with exceptional financial need. The school is the lender with this program.

While there are only two currently active federal loan programs, depending on *when* you went to pharmacy school, you may also have FFEL or Stafford loans. FFEL or Stafford loans can be subsidized or unsubsidized. These loans were no longer issued after 2010.

Loan Servicers

Although federal loans are issued by the Department of Education (DoE), a loan servicer oversees the administration of the loan once it's disbursed by the Department of Education.

The servicer is your main point of contact for handling everything related to your loans, like updating personal information or making a payment on your loan. And just to make things more confusing, you can have multiple servicers by the time the grace period ends and you start repayment.

There are nine federal loan servicers that you may already be familiar with, like Nelnet and Navient. You might have already experienced some frustration dealing with your loan servicer because of poor customer service or the thought of how much money you'll pay in the years to come.

It's important to note that if you chose to do a Direct Consolidation of your federal loans, it takes all of the loans you choose and lumps them into one payment with a weighted interest rate. This allows you to pay one servicer, which is really convenient, and also adds the benefit of unlocking income-driven repayment plans that I'll talk about in detail later.

Inventory Your Private Loans

If you needed to secure funds outside of the federal loan system during your education or have already refinanced your federal student loans, all of your private loans need to be accounted for as well to get an accurate inventory of your debt.

Typically, you can log into your online account with the servicer that handles your loan. However, if you want to confirm, you can do the following.

1. Access your credit report from one of the three major credit bureaus

Go to www.annualcreditreport.com. Please use caution when checking your credit report, as there can be scams to access your personal information. Make sure to only use this website. Through this site, you are able to access a free report once per year from the three reporting agencies: Equifax, TransUnion, and Experian. To make sure you have the most accurate and up-to-date information, reconcile the data on your credit report with the individual lender or bank.

Also, student loan borrowers typically have long credit reports (see CVS receipt joke again) because of how these lenders report student loan debt to the credit bureaus. Typically, it is recorded by disbursement (about once per semester), so try not to get overwhelmed by what you see on your report.

2. Identify your total outstanding balance, interest, and loan servicer

Here we are at that dreaded step again! Take a deep breath and remember that getting those numbers is important so you can formulate a game plan to knock this debt down. After all, like love handles, door-to-door salesmen, and mosquitos, ignoring your loans won't make them disappear.

After you pull your credit report, record your private loan information to give you a full picture of both your federal and private loans.

If the information is not accurate, attempt to resolve the discrepancy by submitting a dispute to the lender servicing the loan. Then, tell the information provider, such as Equifax, TransUnion, or Experian, that you dispute an item on the credit report.

When doing an inventory of all your loans, don't forget to include any balances owed to family members or friends. Uncle Bob deserves to get his money back, too! Just a reminder, include your spouse or significant other's loans, as well.

Now that you have an inventory of your loans and a better understanding of the types of loans you borrowed, let's talk about key payoff strategies.

Chapter 2

THE KEY PAYOFF STRATEGIES

If you go to the www.studentaid.gov website, on one of the pages under the "How to Repay Your Loans" sections it says:

> You must repay your loans even if you don't complete your education, can't find a job related to your program of study, or are unhappy with the education you paid for with your loan. You also can't claim that you have no responsibility for repaying your loan because you were a minor (under the age of 18) when you signed your promissory note or received the loan.

Like the Sugarland song "Stuck like Glue," it's hard to get rid of federal student loans.

Aside from dying or becoming permanently disabled, you're going to have to pay them back or meet the requirements for one of the forgiveness programs.

But probably no surprises there, right?

There are some other rare circumstances where your loans could be discharged, such as your school closes when you are still enrolled or shortly after you withdraw, an unpaid refund by your school, identity theft, or declaring bankruptcy, although the latter is pretty difficult to execute.

You could also get accepted to be on the game show *Paid Off* and win, or you could move to a jungle in India and ride elephants to escape paying.

So, after accepting that you're likely on the hook and there isn't going to be any magic wand to wipe away your debt, it's time to create a plan.

Know Your Options

You heard my story at the beginning of this book and how I failed to fully realize the benefits of PSLF, which ended up costing me over $100,000.

If you walk away with one key piece of advice from this book, it would be to analyze all of your student loan payoff strategies!

I can't stress this enough, as failing to do so can end up costing you big. Once you commit to a particular path, it can be hard to switch course and doing so may come with a price.

That's why you want to be confident in the path you choose.

People often get student loan repayment plans and payoff strategies confused. A repayment plan dictates your minimum payments over a designated term or amount of time. A payoff strategy is your overall game plan that aligns with your goals while saving you the most money. This can be executed using a number of repayment plans, terms, and companies. This is something that you develop for your personal situation and loans.

While there are many plans in both the federal and private system, tuition reimbursement, forgiveness, and non-forgiveness are the major ways to pay off pharmacy school loans.

If you want to quickly get an idea of what might work best for you, check out our student loan quiz at www.yourfinancialpharmacist.com/quiz

Tuition Reimbursement

While not abundantly available, tuition reimbursement or tuition repayment programs essentially provide "free" money, typically from your employer or institution, in exchange for working for a certain period of time.

Pretty awesome, right?

Some programs will require you to pay a certain amount toward your loans and in return you'll be matched or reimbursed.

The ones that tend to provide the most generous reimbursement or repayment are those offered by the federal government through the military, Veterans Health Administration, and the Department of Health.

If you're a pharmacist who works for or plans to work for one of these organizations, you definitely want to check with your human resources department to see if you're eligible. Typically, there is a set amount of funding for these programs, so even if you're not eligible initially, you may be able to reapply in a subsequent year.

There are also many state programs that offer assistance as well. The programs vary in amounts and how payments are structured, so it's important to know all the details to determine how much to pay out of pocket to maximize the total benefit.

Since many of these programs, especially ones through individual states, will not cover your entire student loan bill, you will likely have to combine it with one of the other payoff strategies. You can check out a full list of current state-specific pharmacist tuition repayment programs on our bonus content page at www.pharmdloans.com/#bonus

The major downside of these programs is that you will need to commit to working for a specific employer for a designated time in order to maximize the benefit.

But if you are passionate about the position and working for the company or organization in general, then this really isn't a big deal, especially if you planned to work there anyway.

However, what if you take a job or position mostly for the loan payoff benefits and then decide later that you want to move on? This can put you in a position of having "golden handcuffs." Despite the name, golden handcuffs are no fun.

Before taking a position to receive reimbursement, make sure you know exactly what the commitment entails, and what happens if you back out early.

Here's a rundown of federal tuition reimbursement programs currently available:

Veterans Health Administration – Besides the loan repayment programs offered through the military, one of the most generous federal loan repayment programs is the Education Debt Reduction Program (EDRP) through the Veterans Health Administration (VHA).

Through the program, pharmacists can receive up to $120,000 over a five-year period, with a maximum of $24,000 per year. Unfortunately, this is not always available and depends on the need and difficulty in filling positions. EDRP was not available for my position when I joined the VA, but a number of my colleagues took advantage of it.

Unlike some programs which provide direct student loan repayment, this is a reimbursement program. If you pay $24,000 per year toward your loans, the VA would reimburse you $24,000. If you have a total student loan balance around $240,000, you would essentially be responsible for paying for half, plus any interest.

With balances less than that, it would make sense to make payments less than $24,000/year to enable you to maximize the benefit. Job postings on usajobs.gov usually have this listed for VA positions if available, but always check with human resources if you are interviewing.

Army Pharmacist Health Professions Loan Repayment Program provides up to $120,000 ($40,000 per year over three years) to pharmacists who commit to a period of service when funding is available. Alternatively, there is a Pharmacist Accession Bonus, which is a one-time sign-on bonus of $30,000 paid in a lump sum.

Navy Health Professions Loan Repayment Program offers financial assistance to practicing pharmacists that are qualified for or hold an appointment as a commissioned officer. Assistance amounts vary. To qualify, you must sign a written agreement to serve on active duty for a prescribed time period.

Indian Health Service Loan Repayment Program offers up to $40,000 in exchange for a two-year full-time service commitment working in an Indian health facility or health facilities serving Alaska Native communities. This program can be extended annually if you continue your service until your entire student debt is paid. Currently, there is no maximum established.

Similar to the EDRP, this program is also based on facility and provider-specific needs. If you accept the IHS LRP award, you cannot receive any other awards from any other government entity that also requires a service commitment. You can find job listings that offer the IHS LRP award on usajobs.gov.

National Institutes of Health (NIH) Loan Repayment Program gives up to $50,000 per year to those who take on a two-year commitment to conduct biomedical or behavioral research funded by a nonprofit or government institution.

NHSC Substance Use Disorder Workforce Loan Repayment Program – As a measure to help battle against the unfortunate opioid epidemic, pharmacists were recently added as a qualifying clinician eligible for the NHSC Substance Use Disorder Workforce Loan Repayment Program, with the main goal of assisting in the treatment of substance abuse in rural and underserved areas nationwide. To be eligible, you have to work at an approved NHSC site that provides Substance Use Disorder (SUD) treatment, which includes Opioid Treatment Programs (OTP), Office-based Opioid Treatment (OBOT) Practices, and Non-opioid Outpatient Substance Use Disorder Sites.

In addition, to receive priority funding, you must have a state-issued license or certification to provide SUD treatment. A provider's license or certification to provide SUD treatment must meet the national standard recognized by the National Board of Certified Counselors (NBCC), the Association for Addiction Professionals (NAADAC), or International Certification and Reciprocity Consortium (IC&RC).

There are two different service options available. The first is a three-year full-time commitment (minimum of 40 hours/week and 45 weeks/year), which has an award of $75,000. The part-time option is also a three-year commitment (minimum of 20 hours/week and 45/weeks per year) and has an award of $37,500.

For a full list of available and updated federal reimbursement programs, check out the post at www.yourfinancialpharmacist.com/ultimate.

Public Service Loan Forgiveness (PSLF)

Public Service Loan Forgiveness, also known as PSLF, is a government program designed to encourage graduates to work in the public sector and take on jobs like teaching, nursing, and law enforcement by offering student loan forgiveness after working and paying on the loans for ten years. This is typically the loan forgiveness strategy that gets the most press, usually for all the wrong reasons.

In order to qualify for PSLF, there's a list of criteria that have to be met with precision. The requirements include working for the right type of employer (government, 501(c)(3) non-profit, or some other non-profit organization), having Direct Loans, being in the right repayment plan (income-driven or standard plans), making 120 qualifying payments over 10 years, and being able to prove that all of these stipulations have been met. Then you, the borrower, can apply to receive tax-free forgiveness!

I'll jump into some of the controversy surrounding the program and also look closely at the math and specific details of PSLF in the next chapter.

Non–PSLF Forgiveness

Many pharmacists are under the impression that they have to work for the government or a non-profit in order to be granted a student loan amnesty. Not so fast! Relief is out there, but the terms are slightly less attractive when compared to PSLF.

You may still be in shock if you just heard for the first time that you're able to receive loan forgiveness outside of the PSLF program. What gives? Forgiveness? For anyone?

The cadence for this program is as follows: it doesn't matter who you work for, you still need to have the right kind of loans, be in the right repayment plan (one of the four income-driven plans, which we'll go into detail about later), make the right amount of payments (typically over 20 or 25 years, depending on the type of loan), and then you can apply to receive forgiveness.

That sounds pretty close to the PSLF program, right? However, there are two big differences with non-PSLF forgiveness. First, instead of making qualifying payments over a 10-year period like with PSLF, non-PSLF forgiveness requires payments over a 20- or 25-year period. Second, after making those qualifying payments and finally applying for non-PSLF forgiveness, you'll receive *taxable* forgiveness on the balance of your loans.

I will go into more details about when this may be a good option in Chapter 4.

Non-forgiveness

If tuition reimbursement, PSLF, or non-PSLF forgiveness aren't going to work for your situation, or you decide it's not right for you, what's left is paying off your pharmacy school loans all on your own.

Although it may sound defeating, paying off the loans on your own terms does have a few perks to it. For starters, you won't be set to a timeline, be restricted to working for a specific employer, or have to wait years for forgiveness or reimbursement.

If you have the cash, you could pay them all today! You're also able to extend the payments significantly, generally up to 30 years. You get to be in charge of (for the most part) how long you need to pay back your loans.

Your monthly payments will be dictated based on the repayment plan you're in; however, you are not bound to this amount and can always accelerate paying off your loans by paying more each month. Making extra payments or lump sums to your student loans can affect your overall savings in interest as well as the amount of time it will take for you to pay off your loans.

If you have federal loans and choose to pay off them off early, you can do so through the federal loan program using one of the many repayment plans available.

However, you can also refinance your loans to a private lender with the goal of reducing your interest rate and overall amount paid. I'll lay out all of the various repayment plans and discuss refinancing in more detail in Chapter 5.

Summary

There are quite a few options to pay back your student loans depending on who you work for and the type of loans you have.

That's why I think it helps to think about your options as one of these three broad strategies. In the next couple of chapters, I will take a deep dive into each of these to help you better understand your eligibility and the advantages of pursuing them.

You will notice that there is not a specific chapter on tuition reimbursement. This is because these programs are limited to specific organizations and states, and funding is not always available. For an updated list of these programs currently available, you can go to www.yourfinancialpharmacist .com/ultimate.

Chapter 3

THE PUBLIC SERVICE LOAN FORGIVENESS PROGRAM

Welcome to the jungle, highway to the danger zone, livin' on a prayer, and rock you like a hurricane. These are some of my favorite classic rock hits and are great sing-along songs. Unfortunately, they are also appropriate anthems for many pursuing the Public Service Loan Forgiveness (PSLF) program.

It's honestly hard to find anything positive in the media about the program, especially when 99% of student loan borrowers who apply for PSLF are denied.

Sound familiar?

That's the headline that has been flooding blogs for some time now and can be very discouraging if you're on the path of forgiveness.

In a 2018 report by the Department of Education, 28% of PSLF applicants were rejected because they had missing or incomplete information on their employer certification form. 70% were rejected for not meeting program requirements.

While these "requirements" seem fairly straightforward, the reality is that there are countless ways to make mistakes, with the chief reason being poor administration and oversight of the program.

PSLF was created under the George W. Bush administration via the College Cost Reduction and Access Act of 2007 (CCRAA) to encourage people to take jobs in public service. Since 2017, when the first borrowers became eligible for forgiveness, a number of issues have surfaced.

These range from people thinking they were eligible the whole time but then being ultimately denied, record-keeping mistakes with loan servicers, and political administrations blocking the Consumer Financial Protection Bureau from trying to fix existing problems.

Needless to say, PSLF has gotten a bad rap.

In addition to all of these issues, there has been an ongoing fear that the program will be terminated, changed, or capped so that borrowers can't get the full benefits they were once promised.

Furthermore, at the time of this book's release, there is even a proposed elimination of this program outlined in the government's budget.

That's why many pharmacists ask the question, "Is it even worth it?"

Well before you throw this option out the window and move on, take a look at the math—and actually answer the question.

Consider a single pharmacist who lives within the contiguous U.S., has a student loan balance of $200,000 in Direct Unsubsidized loans with an average interest rate of 7%, an adjusted gross income of $120,000, and 5% income growth per year.

Compared to the 10-year Standard Repayment plan, which results in a monthly payment of $2,322 and a total of $278,660 paid, pursuing PSLF through the income-driven repayment plans REPAYE, PAYE, or IBR-New would result in only $130,657 paid, a difference of almost $150,000!

Plus, the total amount paid could be even lower if the pharmacist were to maximize traditional 401(k) contributions and other options to lower adjusted gross income, since that's how loan payments are calculated under income-based repayment plans.

Oh, and that $209,343 loan balance remaining after 10 years? Forgedda bout it! It's eliminated and there are no taxes to pay on that money.

But beyond the math, think about your lifestyle and other financial goals over the next 10 years.

With the example above, the monthly payment over 10 years would be around $800-$1,300 per month in one of the income-driven repayment plans mentioned.

That's an extra $1,000 or more in your pocket each month compared to the payments in the standard 10-year plan. An extra $1,000 to fund retirement, go on vacations, invest in real estate, or whatever else you want to do. Hard to argue about that benefit, right?

Because it typically results in the lowest monthly payment and the total amount paid, it's often the most beneficial strategy for pharmacists paying off student loans.

PSLF Requirements

If you're somebody who can stomach the rocky past and uncertain future of PSLF, know that it *still* may not be an easy road.

You are going to have to deal with constant negative publicity in the media. Friends, family, and even prominent personal finance figures may be trying to talk you out of it.

You may have to fight against feelings of uneasiness of having loans for 10 years with your balance growing along the way.

And, just a fair warning, you may have to deal with poor service and recordkeeping of the loan servicer, resulting in a number of emails and phone calls to straighten things out.

If you can get past these potential barriers and challenges, here are a number of requirements you need to meet: You need to work for the right type of employer, have the right kind of loans, be in the right repayment plan, make the right amount of payments, and then finally prove it and apply to receive tax-free forgiveness.

Let's jump into each of these requirements and how to execute them in order to avoid mistakes.

Qualified Employment

Types of Employers

Verifying that your employer is a qualifying employer is the first key to the whole process. You don't want to make payments for 10 years only to find out you were ineligible the whole time.

A qualifying employer has to be under one of the three main categories: Government, non-profit 501(c)(3), and not-for-profit that is not tax-exempt under section 501(c)(3) of the IRS code.

Government employers include federal, state, local, or tribal. This includes all branches of the military within the Department of Defense, government public child and family service entities, and also the Peace Corps or Americorps.

This would include pharmacists working for the Department of Veterans Affairs, Department of Health and Human Services through Indian Health Services, Centers for Disease Control and Prevention, Federal Drug Administration, the National Institutes of Health, the Department of Defense through one of the military branches, and the Department of Justice in the Federal Prison Bureau.

Non-profit 501(c)(3) organizations are those that meet the criteria under that specific section of the IRS code. Besides government employment, this is the other major way many pharmacists are eligible, given the number of hospitals and clinics that fall into this category.

The last category of eligible employers, and the least likely path to PSLF for most pharmacists, is non-profit but non-tax-exempt public service. These include emergency management, military service (that does not count under government employment), public safety, law enforcement, public interest legal services, early childhood education, public service for individuals with disabilities and the elderly, public health, public education, public library services, school library services, or other school-based services.

This category for forgiveness is not as black and white as the first two and has actually resulted in lawsuits against the Department of Education, which I'll discuss in a moment.

When you submit your employment certification form to determine your initial eligibility, FedLoan Servicing, the exclusive servicer of PSLF, ultimately makes the call.

A number of attorneys who worked for the American Bar Association, which is considered a non-profit but non-tax-exempt organization, received the initial authorization that they were eligible. They put in their 10 years of service and made their 120 qualifying payments thinking they were on track.

However, when they applied to receive forgiveness, they were surprised and frustrated to find that they were rejected by the Department of Education, which stated their employer did not actually qualify.

Shady, right?

The good news is that these decisions of denial were eventually over-turned—but it took a lot of money and effort to resolve.

This is just one of the many issues that people have faced when committing to the program.

Since working for a qualified employer for 10 years is a core requirement, that will limit some of the flexibility you have with job selection. You can always switch from one qualifying employer to another, but any payments made during a transition period will not count. This is a key consideration to keep in mind if you are fully committed to this program.

Full-Time Employment

Besides having the right employer, you also have to be working full-time based on how your employer defines it or at least 30 hours/week, which-ever is greater.

If you are working part-time for more than one qualifying employer, you can still meet the full-time requirement as long as you are working at least 30 hours per week between the eligible employers.

Filling out the Employment Certification Form

On the PSLF employment certification form, you will have to provide some basic information about your employer, including name, federal employer identification number, address, and the dates that you worked there, and whether it was full- or part-time. You will also have to designate one of the categories that counts as qualified employment.

Lastly, someone from your organization has to sign and provide contact information to attest that you were actually an employee during the documented dates. There is no stipulation on who that individual is from your employer, but it's probably a good idea to pick an immediate supervisor or someone who knows you well in case any questions or discrepancies arise.

Depending on how many qualified employers you work for over 10 years, or however long it takes you to make 120 qualifying payments, you may have to submit multiple certification forms for different employers.

If for some reason you did not fill out the form when you started down the PSLF path and now work for a different employer, but previously made qualifying payments, you can still get credit for those.

Although not required by the program, it's a good idea to re-certify employment annually. Submitting the employment certification form on an annual basis will help confirm you are on track for forgiveness, because FedLoan Servicing will count your qualified payments.

Tim Baker, our Certified Financial Planner™ on the team, often jokes that FedLoan Servicing needs some handholding to appropriately administer the PSLF program, and this is an example! However, despite this, the program can still be worth pursuing.

Qualified Loans

Only federal Direct Loans are eligible for PSLF. This would include all of your federal loans if you're a new borrower after July 1, 2010, which come in the form of Direct Unsubsidized, Direct Subsidized, Direct Consolidation, and Direct PLUS loans.

If you borrowed before that time, you may have Family Federal Education or FFEL Loans. These, including Perkins loans, are technically ineligible and any payments you made on these will not count toward PSLF.

However, there is a loophole. If you perform a Direct Consolidation Loan with any of these older loans, you unlock eligibility by enabling the qualifying income-driven repayment plans, and all payments moving forward would qualify.

The one exception to this is Parent PLUS loans. The only income-driven repayment plan eligible for these after a Direct Consolidation Loan is the ICR, or Income-Contingent plan, so you can't lump all of your other loans with it.

Although, generally, this is not the preferred income-driven repayment plan for PSLF, it's a way to make these loans eligible. If Parent PLUS loans constitute just a part of your overall loan balance, it's possible you could have two different PSLF timelines.

Take caution with this step of consolidation! If you've been making standard 10-year or income-driven payments on any Direct Loan while working for a qualifying employer and you decide to consolidate these in addition to FFEL or Perkins loans, you're essentially hitting the reset button on your PSLF timeline and starting your 10-year period anew.

Just to repeat: Do not consolidate any Direct Loans that you have already made qualifying payments on.

Therefore, you may have to designate specific loans to be consolidated vs. consolidating all of them, which will create multiple PSLF timelines.

Private loans are not eligible under any circumstances. That's why if you are thinking about refinancing, make sure you're confident PSLF is not an option or the best option, since you will automatically disqualify yourself once you make that move—just like I did!

After you verify your loans are eligible or finalize the consolidation process, you and your employer need to complete the PSLF employment certification form.

If you are a new graduate and in the grace period, it's a great idea to apply for the Direct Consolidation Loan to combine all your loans into one and ensure they are eligible to avoid any possible mistakes.

Qualifying Monthly Payments

You have to make 120 qualified payments prior to receiving forgiveness. "Qualified" here means that double or extra payments will not count! Therefore, you can't make the process go any faster than 10 years. You are locked in for a decade.

While that may seem depressing, remember the benefits!

Later on, I'll talk about how to maximize your investments while in the program.

So, once you've acknowledged that you're in this for at least 10 years, you can create a cool art project with 120 checks, notches, or color-in areas to celebrate your progress.

While you can't make extra payments, you also can't make payments for less than the bill amount. I'm sure that's not surprising, right?

Besides paying the full amount, your payments have to be on time, as anything paid more than 15 days past the due date will not count. To avoid this from ever being an issue, consider putting your payments on automatic withdrawal.

In addition, the payments have to be made when you are in *active repayment*. Any payments made during the grace period, deferment, or forbearance will not count.

One key point is that these payments do not have to be consecutive. If you have to switch jobs from one qualifying employer to another and there is a gap in employment, you can pick back up where you left off when you start working again.

Another possible scenario that has unfortunately occurred is an employer such as a hospital could change its non-profit status. By making this change, it would automatically make any payments from that point forward ineligible.

Obviously, that would be a reason to make a job transition to another qualifying employer if you still want to achieve forgiveness.

Qualifying Repayment Plans

Only payments under a qualifying repayment plan count toward your 120. These include income-based repayment (IBR), income-contingent repayment (ICR), Pay-as-you-earn (PAYE), Revised-pay-as-you-earn (REPAYE), and payments under the 10-year Standard Repayment Plan.

Even though the 10-year Standard Repayment plan technically is an option, do not do this! It makes no sense since your goal of PSLF is to pay the least amount you are legally obligated to over 10 years. Staying in this repayment program for the duration would accomplish the complete opposite.

However, if you have erroneously made payments through this plan and are now in the process of optimizing PSLF, remember they will still count. If that's you, get moving and switch your repayment plan ASAP!

One important note is that the Standard Repayment Plan for Direct Consolidation Loans is not the same repayment plan as the 10-Year Standard Repayment Plan. Payments made under the Standard Repayment Plan for Direct Consolidation Loans do not usually qualify for PSLF purposes.

How Payments are Calculated

The plans that will result in the lowest monthly payments are REPAYE, PAYE, and IBR-New (which functions essentially the same as PAYE), since they are calculated as 10% of your discretionary income.

For these plans, discretionary income is specifically your adjusted gross income minus 150% of the poverty guidelines. The U.S. poverty guidelines are set by the Department of Health and Human Services and help determine eligibility for certain federal programs.

These incorporate family size and are updated annually for inflation using the consumer price index. These guidelines are the same for all states, with the exceptions of Alaska and Hawaii, which have higher limits.

Here's an example of how your payment would be calculated if you lived anywhere besides Alaska or Hawaii. If you are single with no dependents, the poverty guideline for 2020 is $12,760. 150% of that number is $19,140. If your adjusted gross income is $120,000, your discretionary income would be $100,860.

Then you take 10% of that number, which is $10,086. Dividing by 12 results in a monthly payment of $841.

At the time of applying for an income-driven repayment plan, you will need to document your income based on last year's tax return. Formerly, you were required to do an annual recertification to document any changes in your income from the previous year.

However, as of December 2019, the U.S. Department of Education and Congress have made some changes to this process with the FUTURES Act.

A part of this bill showcases a new data-sharing agreement between the Internal Revenue Service (IRS) and the U.S. Department of Education. Instead of having to recertify to stay on an income-driven repayment plan like before, borrowers can have their plans automatically renewed every year based on their tax return.

Without an automated process, borrowers could have been paying additional, costly interest or missing student loan forgiveness payments if a recertification application was late or forgotten.

This process should be a positive change and increase the accuracy of documentation. However, as always, you'll want to be sure that errors aren't made and that your tax return is accurately shared if you opt in to this option.

Reporting Income

Previously, the income-driven repayment form asked the question, "Has your income significantly increased or decreased since you filed your last federal income tax return?" This was really confusing, as there was no guidance on what constituted "significant."

However, this has changed and now only asks if your pay has significantly decreased since the last tax filing.

This is a big deal, especially if you are a resident or fellow transitioning from student life or from resident to new practitioner, since your payments will be based on last year's income.

If you are a PGY1, you would be documenting income you had as a student. As a PGY2, you would document income as a PGY1, and as a new practitioner you would document income from your previous year of residency.

Even if you didn't complete a residency or fellowship and went straight into a pharmacist position that qualifies for PSLF, your first year of payments would be based on the income you had as a student.

Therefore, you are going to pay substantially less during your transition years, which is another huge perk of this program.

Of course, you want to be truthful and accurate when filling out the form, but if you are not required to disclose increases in your income, then you shouldn't. Why not take full advantage of the system in place?

If you opt in for data-sharing of your tax information based on the FUTURES Act, then you may only have to fill this out in your initial income-driven repayment application.

Choosing the Best Repayment Plan

Now the main question becomes, "Which of the repayment plans is best for PSLF?" or, better, "Which of the repayment plans will result in the least amount paid over 10 years?"

You may be thinking "Does it really matter?" since I noted that the plans I mentioned earlier require you to pay 10% of your discretionary income.

If only it were that simple! You can go ahead and check off another box in the "why PSLF is frustrating" list.

In general, the best repayment plan will depend on your income, marital status, spouse's income, and when your loans were disbursed.

Without getting into the weeds, let me try to make things as simple as possible.

Most people should choose PAYE. As mentioned above, this repayment plan will cap your payments at 10% of your discretionary income and you will never pay more than that amount for the 10-year standard repayment plan.

In addition, you only have to incorporate your spouse's income if you file a joint return, which gives you some flexibility if you need to change filing status during the 10 years. IBR-New essentially functions the exact same way as PAYE, with the exception that you have to have loans disbursed on or after July 1, 2014.

Initially, to qualify for PAYE, you must have been a new borrower on or after October 1, 2007 and also received a disbursement of a Direct Loan or FFEL on or after October 1, 2011. This generally won't be an issue if you are a new graduate or a graduate within the last decade.

Besides that, for PAYE, your calculated payment based on your income has to be less than what you would pay for the 10-year Standard Plan. Based on typical student loan debt and starting pharmacist salaries, this also typically won't be a problem.

During the 10 years you are making payments, you have to recertify your income annually. If your income happens to increase either because of your own efforts or spouse's to the point where payments would match or exceed the 10-year Standard Plan, it is possible that you could be told or persuaded by your servicer to change to REPAYE.

The problem with this is that under REPAYE, you can actually pay MORE than the standard 10-year payment. Again, your goal is to pay the least amount of money.

If you ever get in that situation, insist to FedLoan Servicing to remain in PAYE or IBR-New and cap your payments at whatever the 10-year standard payments would be. In other words, at least under the current program guidelines, no matter how much money you earn, you cannot be disqualified from the program or be forced into REPAYE.

If you've been out of school for a while and don't qualify for PAYE or IBR-New, then you're stuck with either REPAYE or IBR. REPAYE would then be the way to go, given you would be paying only 10% of your discretionary income vs. 15% with IBR.

The only exception to go with IBR would be if you're married and there was a significant advantage to filing your taxes separately, since this is not an option with REPAYE.

To figure out the repayment strategy for PSLF that will save you the most money, you can use the Loan Simulator at www.studentaid.gov/loan-simulator. This will take into account your loan balance, income, spouse's income, income growth, and family size. You can also add in retirement contributions to a traditional employer-sponsored plan and/or HSA (Health Savings Account). This tool will estimate your monthly payments, the total amount paid, and the amount forgiven over ten years.

The best practice to confirm your qualifying payments is to submit the employment certification form annually so there are no surprises at the end of the 10-year repayment period. FedLoan will respond to your annual submissions via letter, detailing the number of qualifying payments you've made thus far.

Make sure you call them out if there are any inaccuracies. Unfortunately, this has been reported to happen often, so you want to ensure you get credit for *all* your qualifying payments.

How to File Your Taxes if You're Married

When you're married and you and or your spouse are pursuing PSLF (or even non-PSLF) forgiveness, filing your taxes separately could make sense.

Since your payments are calculated based on AGI, assuming your spouse has an income, filing jointly would generally result in bigger loan payments. Although filing separately would lower the payment, you would also get a lower tax deduction than you would if you filed jointly.

Therefore, the only time filing separately would be beneficial is if your savings with your payments is greater than the lost tax deduction. You can do some projections with tax software to estimate the potential benefit, but you may want to defer to a financial planner or tax expert who is familiar with loan forgiveness.

This is something that the YFP financial planning team handles all the time, so if you want to reach out and set up an appointment, you can go to www.yourfinancialpharmacist.com/planning.

Remember this is only an option for PAYE, IBR, or ICR. Payments through REPAYE will count spousal income regardless of how you file.

If you file your taxes jointly and both you and your spouse have federal student loans, your servicer should automatically adjust your payment amount proportionally based on each spouse's share of the debt. For example, if you are in PAYE and the total payment amount based on joint income is $1,000, and your debt is 70% of the total balance, your payment would be $700 and your spouse's payment would be $300.

Another situation that is a little more complex is if you file taxes separately and live in a community property state. These include Louisiana, Arizona, Texas, Washington, Idaho, Nevada, New Mexico, and Wisconsin.

Essentially, when you're married and live in a community property state, you and your spouse own marital property as an even 50/50 split, and this includes income and debt. These states require that the incomes are combined and split evenly for federal tax reporting. So you may have to submit alternative documentation to your loan servicer to show individual incomes to determine the basis for income-driven payments.

Applying for Forgiveness

Once you have made all of your 120 qualifying payments, you still haven't made it to the finish line.

"Seriously!?"

There's still one more step. You have to actually apply for forgiveness with another form, called the PSLF Application for Forgiveness, which can be uploaded directly to the FedLoan Servicing website.

Once submitted, you can cross your fingers and hold your breath as it is reviewed. Hopefully, you finally will receive tax-free forgiveness.

The time it takes to receive notification about your application will vary based on how complex your employment history is, whether there are gaps in payments, and whether you previously submitted employment certification forms. As Tom Petty said, "The waiting is the hardest part."

If for some reason you did not submit any Employment Certification Forms prior to submitting your PSLF application, or if you submitted forms for only some of your employers for only a portion of your period of qualifying employment, you will need to provide one or more Employment Certification Forms, as necessary, to cover your entire period of qualifying employment (including your current employment).

This is the main reason I recommended to submit the employment certification form from the very beginning and continue to submit it annually so that your loan(s) will already be serviced by FedLoan and your payments will be tracked. This will simplify the process at the very end. In addition, as indicated on the Department of Education website, the time to get approved will likely be a lot faster.

Another important consideration when submitting your PSLF Application for Forgiveness is to make sure you are still working for a qualified employer at the time you submit this form.

This is another requirement and therefore another opportunity to make a mistake. Although you may be tempted and ready to move from your current position after you make the 120th payment, hold out a little longer!

Other PSLF Considerations

After hearing all of these steps, I wouldn't be surprised if you're feeling pretty overwhelmed. It's a complex process with many opportunities to make mistakes.

Aside from that and the past mishaps with this program, you have to look to the future with a measure of concern, too. Usually, when we talk risk related to financial matters, it involves the risk you take with your investments, whether it be market risk or interest rate risk.

However, borrowers who enroll and put their proverbial eggs in the PSLF basket take on legislative risk or the risk that laws could change. This program is at the whim of the President and Congress, which may not allow you to sleep easy at night.

Based on the language in past proposals to eliminate or cap the PSLF program, it is likely that any change will merely affect *future* borrowers and not those currently enrolled in the PSLF program. This is based on the fact that Congress allocated a sizeable sum of money for those "oops" situations called Temporary Expanded Public Service Loan Forgiveness (TEPLSF).

In March 2018, the Department of Education announced this program to aid those borrowers who thought they were on the path to forgiveness but were ultimately denied when they applied after their 10 years of repayment.

The reconsideration fund allocated by Congress, totaling $350M, should provide relief for those borrowers who thought they took the necessary steps to achieve PSLF but fell short for one reason or another.

This is on a first-come basis and, as mentioned, is temporary, so if you feel you are in this situation, you can go to studentloans.gov, review the criteria, and send an email for reconsideration of your rejected PSLF application.

Lastly, many borrowers who seek this strategy often see their loans grow over their PSLF timeline despite making qualifying payments. For that hypothetical borrower who is halfway through their PSLF timeline but has seen the balance balloon because of reduced income-driven payments, would the government actually issue a legislative "sike...just kidding" for the loan forgiveness program and not grandfather that borrower in?

It's not out of the realm of possibility, but the political fallout that would ensue for many of those in public service would be a steep price to pay. Again, it's a risk you have to consider when looking at your options.

Optimizing Your PSLF Strategy

Aside from crossing your T's and dotting your I's with every single requirement in the program, there's a way to maximize your benefits.

Since your payments in PSLF are determined by your adjusted gross income (AGI), lowering that amount would, in turn, lower your payments over the 10 years and minimize the amount you are responsible for.

The most beneficial way to do this is to max out your traditional 401(k), 403(b), most 457 plans, or Thrift Savings plan. This will lower your AGI and reduce monthly payments while simultaneously growing investments. Pretty cool, right?

Let's say you maxed out your 401k every year for 10 years while in PSLF. Assuming a 1% raise in income each year with a typical pharmacist salary and no employer match, and a net rate of return of 5%, you have a whopping $250,000. Having a quarter of a million dollars in investments and no more student loan debt wouldn't be such a bad position to be in, right?

Assuming you are enrolled in a high deductible health plan, contributing to a Health Savings Account would also lower your student loan payments, although to a much lesser extent than a 401(k), given the contribution limits. However, HSAs are a great way to save for retirement, given the triple tax benefits they have.

There are also some other adjustments you may be eligible for which could lower your AGI and are on schedule 1 of the 1040 tax form. Because of the income limits, most pharmacists will not be able to deduct student loan interest or contributions to an IRA unless you are a resident or fellow.

If you've listened to me on the side hustle series on the YFP podcast and followed my advice there, you might even be eligible to contribute to something called a SEP IRA. This is typically an IRA for self-employed individuals that offers a larger contribution amount than a traditional IRA or even a 401(k), depending on the earnings. These contributions also lower your AGI.

Overall, this is one of the most attractive features of the program and it eliminates the question of whether to invest while paying off student loans since it's so advantageous to do both.

Summary

You could say that all the stars have to be aligned in order to actually make it all the way through the PSLF requirements and receive forgiveness. I told you it's not an easy journey, but it can be totally worth it.

Since there was a lot of information in this chapter, I want to summarize the steps you need to take from start to finish.

Step 1. Confirm employment eligibility.

Step 2. Confirm loan eligibility. If all loans are direct loans, then perform a Direct Consolidation Loan if you are about to enter repayment for the first time.

Step 3. Submit the Employment Certification Form. If accepted, your loans will be consolidated and transferred to FedLoan Servicing, the exclusive servicer for PSLF.

Step 4. Choose the best income-driven repayment plan. This will be PAYE for most. You will need to opt in one time to allow the IRS to share your tax returns with the U.S. Department of Education. This eliminates the need to recertify your income annually on the income-driven repayment plan.

Step 5. Reduce your Adjusted Gross Income through retirement contributions. Traditional contributions made to your 401(k) and/or HSA will lower your taxable income and, in turn, lower your payments as you invest.

Step 6. Re-certify employment annually. Submitting the employment certification form on an annual basis will help confirm you are on track for forgiveness and FedLoan Servicing will count your qualified payments. You will also have to submit this form any time you change to a different qualifying employer.

Step 7. Apply for forgiveness after making 120 qualifying payments. The PSLF Application for Forgiveness must be submitted while you are still working for a qualified employer. If accepted, your loan balance will be forgiven tax-free.

The Department of Education now has a PSLF Help Tool at www.studentaid.gov that allows you to log in to your account and the tool will walk you through the PSLF process and help determine your eligibility. You can also find the forms you need to start or complete the process there.

If you still need more guidance about PSLF and want to make sure you're on track to receive forgiveness, you can reach out to one of our Certified Financial Planners™ on the Your Financial Pharmacist team at www.yourfinancialpharmacist.com/planning.

Chapter 4

NON-PSLF FORGIVENESS

If you're not eligible for PSLF, you may be thinking that your only other option to improve your student loan situation is to refinance and call it a day. Not so fast!

Forgiveness is out there, albeit with less attractive terms. However, if you're someone with a huge debt load that far exceeds your income, this can be an awesome option.

The cadence for this program is similar to PSLF in that you still need to have federal Direct Student Loans and be in a qualifying income-driven repayment plan, but there are a few differences. It doesn't matter who you work for, and you will need to make payments over 20 or 25 years, depending on the type of loan. Once these qualifications are met, you can apply to receive taxable, rather than tax-free, forgiveness.

Aside from the term and no employer requirement, the taxable forgiveness versus the tax-free forgiveness is actually a big deal. Let me explain why.

In the PSLF program, if after making 120 qualified payments you have a balance of $100,000 when you apply for forgiveness, Hakuna Matata! It means no worries, for that balance is forgiven!

For non-PSLF forgiveness, if you have a $100,000 balance forgiven at the end of 20 years, that $100,000 is viewed as taxable income.

That means that if your estimated tax responsibility is ⅓ of the amount forgiven, you'll owe an additional $33,000 in taxes in the year following forgiveness. Often referred to as a "tax bomb," it's something that non-PSLF forgiveness borrowers need to account for, typically by saving or investing concurrently to making student loan payments.

Although the length of repayment and the tax bomb can make this strategy unattractive to some, there are some situations where it can make a lot of sense.

Depending on your cost of living, liabilities, and other financial responsibilities, it could be very difficult to make non-income-driven payments through the standard plan, extended plans, or even the terms offered with refinancing.

Let's walk through an example.

Assumptions: Single, all loans are unsubsidized and qualify for PAYE, an average interest rate of 7%, yearly income increase of 5%, and an overall federal tax responsibility of 33% based on today's tax law and average pharmacist earnings. This example does not take into account state income tax, which ranges from 0 to 10%.

If you had a total loan balance of $375,000 and you divide your income of, let's say, $120,000, your debt-to-income ratio is ~3:1. Through the 10-year standard repayment plan, you would have to make payments of about $3,500 per month.

Wow! That's a pretty hefty payment, right? Maybe even impossible given your situation.

To lower your payments, you would likely be compelled to opt for a longer term, such as the extended fixed repayment plan, where you make fixed payments over 25 years. You could also refinance to lower your interest and therefore lower your payment. Or you could opt for non-PSLF forgiveness after 20 years through an income-driven repayment plan.

Let's look at how each of these scenarios would play out in terms of monthly payments, total amount paid, and the potential tax responsibility. We will assume the refinanced rate is fixed at 4%.

Scenario 1. Extended fixed repayment plan
- Term: 25 years
- Monthly Payment: $2,650
- Total Amount Paid: $795,126

Scenario 2. Refinance to 4% Fixed Interest Rate
- Term: 20 years

- Monthly Payment: $2,851
- Total Amount Paid: $545,382

Scenario 3. Non-PSLF forgiveness via PAYE

- Term: 20 years
- Monthly Payment: Ranges from $844 to $2,120
- Total Amount Paid: $349,496
- Total Amount Forgiven: $550,504
- Total Tax Bill After Forgiveness: $181,666
- Total Amount Paid + Tax Bill: $531,162

Based on these estimations there are significant advantages to seeking non-PSLF forgiveness.

First, the total amount paid over 20 years will be much less, even with considering the additional tax bill, by almost $200,000 compared to the 25-year extended fixed repayment plan, and by about $15,000 compared to refinancing to a 4% interest rate.

However, even this is a very conservative estimation since this comparison would assume that you had to save every dollar for the tax bomb. With 20 years to save $181,666, assuming you invested a monthly amount $446 and achieved a net rate of return of 5% over 20 years, you would only be paying $107,040, or about half the actual amount. With this estimation the total amount paid via non-PSLF forgiveness would be $88,846 cheaper than refinancing the loan to a 20-year term at 4% fixed interest.

Definitely not a small chunk of change. That's well worth dealing with the tax bomb!

Next, for many of the years during repayment, the monthly payments through PAYE will be significantly lower compared to the alternatives, which yields more disposable income. This gives you significantly more breathing room to fund retirement contributions, contribute toward other financial goals, and just live life in general.

Lastly, you have to think of the tax bill of $181,666 in future value. That amount in 20 years is going to be less than what it is worth today.

Are You a Candidate?

As mentioned, pharmacists most likely to benefit from this program are those with high debt-to-income ratios who don't qualify for PSLF. Typically, this is somewhere around 2:1 or higher, meaning your student loan debt is at least twice your annual income.

If your debt-to-income ratio is closer to 1:1, this strategy doesn't make sense. That's because your loans will be paid off before 20 to 25 years have elapsed, so income-driven repayments will result in no amount forgiven.

So, what is the magic number?

The easiest way to see if this is a good option is to run your own numbers through those scenarios in the example we discussed.

To determine your estimated payments and the amount forgiven, you can use the loan simulator at studentaid.gov. Although it can help give you a reasonable estimate, there are some notable limitations.

It won't take into account transition years when going from a resident or fellow salary to a practicing pharmacist.

In addition, you don't get the option to change your marital status, how you file your taxes, or the number of dependents during each year of loan repayment. The projections from the estimator assumes that these variables don't change for 20 to 25 years.

If you want to be able to manipulate all of these variables during your years of repayment, I suggest checking out the calculator at www.studentloanplanner.com

To run scenarios with different refinance rates, check out our calculator at www.yourfinancialpharmacist.com/refinance-calculator and you can enter the rates you have been initially approved for.

Choosing the Best Repayment Plan

Similar to PSLF, you have multiple income-driven repayment options to choose from, including PAYE, REPAYE, IBR, IBR-New, and ICR.

The main difference between them is how your payment is calculated and when forgiveness kicks in. Remember, for PAYE, REPAYE, and IBR-NEW, your payments are 10% of your discretionary income, 15% for IBR, and the lesser of 20% of discretionary income or the payment for a 12-year fixed payment for ICR.

PAYE will result in forgiveness after 20 years, or 240 qualifying income-driven payments. This is the same for IBR-New. With either of these plans, you also get the option to file your taxes separately if married, which could be beneficial. And you will never pay more than the payment for the standard 10-year plan.

For some tips on when to consider filing taxes separately, refer to chapter 3.

The time to forgiveness with REPAYE is 20 years if you were paying back strictly undergraduate loans otherwise it's 25 years. It's also 25 years for IBR or ICR.

Again, let's just make things as simple as possible. Similar to PSLF, PAYE will likely be the best move assuming you are eligible, mainly because of the timeline and the option to file your taxes separately, if advantageous.

How to Prepare for the Tax Bomb

Depending on how big your student loan debt is, you may be expecting a pretty significant tax liability in 20 to 25 years when you're on the non-PSLF forgiveness path. Remember, because you are only making income-driven payments, your student loan balance is likely going to grow over time. And we're not talking about just a slight increase.

The total amount forgiven could end up being larger than the original balance you started paying on!

That can be overwhelming and is one of the reasons people avoid this payoff strategy.

The good news is that you have several years to prepare and you have options.

It's impossible to know exactly what your tax rate will be in 20 to 25 years. You could base your estimation on what today's rates are and assume that your income increases over time would evenly offset any change. Or you could plan for a higher rate to be more conservative.

You're probably thinking, "What is the best way to save for the tax bomb?"

You could simply use a basic checking or savings account, project your tax responsibility, and then divide that amount over the years remaining until forgiveness.

If you think you are going to owe an additional $100,000 in 20 years, you would simply save $5,000 per year.

But you have other options as well, such as a high-yield savings account. Although rates vary, typically you can get a 1 to 2% return. Assuming the bank or company is FDIC insured, you would have virtually no risk of losing money and would not have to pay as much out of pocket over 20 years.

For the example above of $100,000, assuming your net rate of return was 2% over 20 years, you would only have to save $4,068 per year.

But what if you were willing to add in a little more risk to the equation and could get an even higher rate of return?

As you know, there is a lot of volatility in the stock market and it's definitely not a great short-term savings option. But it does have a pretty good track record over a 20-year period. Tim Baker often jokes that outside of the zombie apocalypse, the market always goes up in the long term. In fact, from 1872 to 2018, the stock market has never had a negative rolling 20-year period. Think about that!

(And hey, in the event of a zombie apocalypse, you'll have bigger problems than your debts to think about!)

So now let's assume that instead of a high-yield savings account, you use a stock index fund that tracks the S&P 500. Historic rates of return over this time frame are typically around 10%. But accounting for inflation, let's go even more conservative at 6%. How much would you need to save to accomplish accumulating $100,000 after 20 years?

In order to reach your goal, you would only need to save $216 per month, or $2,592 per year. Basically, half of the actual amount in this case. That's a lot more manageable to think about and plan for.

The best way to ensure you are on track to hit this goal is to automate your savings. Just think of it as part of the student loan payment you are responsible for.

You can calculate the amount you need to save to prepare for your tax liability by using our savings goal calculator at www.yourfinancialpharmacist.com/savings-goal-calculator.

In the examples above, the tax responsibility was based on federal taxes only. If you live in a state such as California, then you would have to plan for an additional 10% of the amount forgiven. If you wanted to avoid this, you could establish residence in a state which has no state income tax prior to the year the loan is forgiven. These include Florida, Texas, Nevada, South Dakota, Washington, Alaska, Wyoming, New Hampshire, or Tennessee.

Tax Season Arrives

When you are filing your taxes in the year following forgiveness after 20 to 25 years, you will report the amount forgiven on form 1099-c, also called "Cancellation of Debt" or COD income. That amount will be counted as taxable income.

You may be thinking, "Is there any way around this?"

The answer is that it depends on your assets at the time your tax bill is due.

In the IRS code, there is something called the insolvency exclusion, where forgiven debt can be excluded as income. But in order for this to occur, you have to meet the IRS definition of insolvent, which is when your total liabilities exceed your total assets.

Your assets are things of value, including a home, car, savings, and retirement accounts, whereas liabilities include credit card debt and car loans in addition to forgiven student loans.

But this does not have to be an all-or-none situation and partial insolvency could occur.

Let's look at an example. If you were on the path of non-PSLF forgiveness and, after 20 years, had accrued a total of $300,000 in assets through your primary residence and retirement accounts and a student loan amount forgiven of $370,000, how much of that would you be responsible for?

Your insolvency number is $70,000, and, since the student loan debt is greater than that, the amount you would be responsible for is $300,000.

According to tax planning attorney Steven Chung, some people may intentionally try to claim insolvency through various strategies to minimize their assets.

Even if you are able to eliminate or minimize the COD bill, there can be many drawbacks to this. First, you are likely going to have low cash on hand and could be in a bad position to pay off any debts other than student loans directly after forgiveness.

Most importantly, the IRS could look at your asset minimizing moves as sham transactions, where the sole intent was to reduce tax liability. An auditor could review these and look for assets being regifted to you post-forgiveness and reclassify them as assets.

The bottom line is that if you are even considering insolvency as a means to mitigate the tax bomb, you definitely want to be working with an experienced tax professional and/or financial planner who is also an expert with student loan management.

Summary

Non-PSLF forgiveness makes the most sense for those with a high debt-to-income ratio and can be cheaper than refinancing to a similar term of 20 years or more.

In addition, payments will be much more manageable and allow room in your budget to achieve other financial goals.

The main downside is that you're locked in for 20 to 25 years and you have to prepare for a potentially large tax bill, since any amount forgiven is treated as income.

Chapter 5

NON-FORGIVENESS AND REFINANCING

Have you been down the frozen food aisle at the grocery store to get some ice cream or frozen yogurt?

Unless you know exactly what you're looking for, the selection can be extremely overwhelming and even paralyzing!

Not only do you have different types of ice cream such as gelato, custard, frozen yogurt, and dairy-free options, you have multiple brands and flavors within each of these categories.

I'll admit I've spent a gratuitous amount of time trying to choose on a number of occasions and often will just go with something that is tried and true.

Outside of tuition reimbursement and forgiveness programs, choosing your student loan strategy can be somewhat similar (but maybe not as sweet!).

You are going to be faced with multiple repayment plans, terms, types of interest rates, and companies. Not only that, but these can change through the life of the loan as well.

While it can be overwhelming, the good news is that the strategy of non-forgiveness gives you the most control over your loans.

The non-forgiveness strategy is a catch-all term for all the other ways to pay off student loans aside from various forgiveness options.

I know, really creative right?

With non-forgiveness, there's no set timeline. There are no ridiculous rules or requirements you have to follow aside from making the minimum payments.

You have the power!

You determine the timeframe to pay off your loans.

You could pay off the balance today if you have the cash or extend payments as long as possible (generally as long as 30 years).

You make it happen when it's best for you.

That's why *repayment plans* and terms are somewhat irrelevant outside of forgiveness.

Yes, your minimum monthly payments will be dictated based on the repayment plan you're in, but you are not bound to this and can always accelerate and pay more if you want to, since there is rarely ever a prepayment penalty.

Within the non-forgiveness strategy, you essentially have two overarching options. Assuming you have federal student loans, you can keep your loans in the federal system or refinance them with a private lender.

Then, within each of those options, you have sub-options with regards to terms, repayment plans, and types of interest rates.

Let's go through these and discuss the options within. In chapter 7, I'll go into more detail about how to choose the timeline that works best for you.

Federal Student Loan Program

If you're like most pharmacists, you probably took out federal student loans to fund pharmacy school and will be handled by one or more of the federal servicers, including Nelnet, Great Lakes Education Loan Services Inc., Navient, FedLoan Servicing, MOHELA, HESC/EdFinancial, Cornerstone, GraniteState, and OSLA.

Some of these companies may also service private loans. Refer to your NSLDS information at www.studenaid.gov for the most accurate list of your federal loans.

If your grace period is up or you have already started making payments, then you, unfortunately, are quite familiar with these names.

Since it is possible to have multiple servicers, you may be making multiple monthly payments to different servicers each month.

If you're in this situation, you could use a Direct Consolidation Loan to combine all of these loans into one and then make one monthly payment to one lender. This option takes the weighted interest rate of all of your loans and will not lower the overall interest rate, as refinancing could.

It just makes things more convenient. Nothing wrong with that.

Repayment Plans

Once the grace period is up, the default loan repayment plan is the standard 10-year plan, where you make the same monthly payment over 10 years. It's the most aggressive of all the federal repayment plans and you will pay less in total interest than the others. Again, you can make more than the minimum payment and pay it off even faster.

Additionally, there is a graduated 10-year plan, where your payments start out low and then increase every two years. This plan also achieves the same result of a zero balance after 10 years.

Similar to the standard plan, the extended repayment plan also comes in two flavors: fixed and graduated. Both types last 25 years instead of 10.

Through a Direct Consolidation Loan, these repayment options are similar, with the caveat that you can extend your loans up to a 30-year term either by making fixed or graduated payments.

Besides these options, you also have access to the income-driven repayment plans (depending on the type of federal loans you have) outlined in the previous forgiveness chapters.

Advantages of the Federal Loan System

Keeping your loans in the federal system will give you some protection and safeguards that are not always available through private lenders.

If you die or become permanently disabled, your loans will be discharged without any tax bill on that amount.

In addition, if you're facing a financial hardship, want to go back to school, or have circumstances where it could be tough to make payments, you can request deferment or forbearance, which would temporarily stop payments.

The other advantage is the ability to make income-driven payments, if needed, which generally is not available through private lenders.

Lastly, all federal loans have fixed interest rates, so your monthly payments will not change unless you are in an income-driven plan or one of the graduated plans.

Disadvantages of the Federal Loan System

One of the biggest issues with keeping your loans in the federal system is that you have no control over the interest rate. Well, at least for now.

There is some legislative discussion about this, but at the time of this audiobook being released, refinancing is not an option within the federal loan program.

And that's kind of a big deal since for your PharmD program, interest on your Direct Loans is likely in the realm of 6-8%.

Again, you can use a Direct Consolidation Loan to combine multiple loans and create a single weighted interest rate. However, the *effective rate* does not change.

If you keep your loans in the federal system, you are stuck with whatever rates you have.

Another disadvantage is that you generally cannot change your federal loan servicer. So, if you're getting poor service and want to make a move, your only option is to use a Direct Consolidation Loan and choose the servicer you want. But this is basically a one-time deal.

Private Lending / Refinancing

Throughout the life cycle of my wife's student loans in addition to my own, we had a total of four different private loan servicers.

Because it's a competitive market with interest rates always changing, we were able to refinance multiple times to continually get a better rate.

Over the course of our payoff, we were able to save thousands of dollars, which couldn't have been accomplished in the federal loan program.

Advantages of Refinancing

When you refinance student loans, you reorganize or change the terms of an existing loan(s). These include the time over which you pay back, the interest rate, the type of interest rate, or a combination of those.

Savings

Consider a pharmacist with $200,000 in student loans carrying a 6.8% overall interest rate. Under the standard 10-year plan, the total amount paid would be $276,192. If the interest rate was chopped to 4%, the total paid would be $242,988, a savings of over $33,000.

The total savings will vary based on the loan balance, how fast it's paid off, and the change in interest rate. If you want to see your potential savings, check out our refinance calculator at www.yourfinancialpharmacist. com/refinance.

Lower Monthly Payments

Another advantage of refinancing could be to lower your monthly payment. Since your total balance will not change at the time of refinancing, if you keep the same term (e.g., 10 years) but lower the interest rate, your payments will go down since a greater percentage of the payment will go toward the principal and less to interest.

For example, let's say you started making a monthly payment of $1,973 through the standard 10-year repayment plan for a loan balance of $170,000 with a 7% interest rate.

If you were able to refinance that rate to 4%, your monthly payment would go down to $1,721, a savings of about $250 per month.

Catalyze Payoff

It's also possible that refinancing your loans could increase your monthly payments. And that *can* be a good thing in some cases!

At one point when I refinanced my loans, my minimum payment went from about $1,000/month to $2,700/month.

In order to get the best interest rate, I had to refinance to a five-year term, resulting in that big monthly payment. However, that wasn't the only reason for this move.

I was on a mission to get rid of my loans as fast as possible and wanted to eliminate one of the biggest barriers to my progress: myself.

When my monthly payments were $1,000, I had some disposable income in my budget and could have paid extra on the loans.

But do you think I did that every month? Of course not. I spent it!

Being forced to make $2,700 monthly payments on auto-draft minimized the opportunity to spend money on things that were not consistent with my big financial goals.

Refinancing jump-started my payoff and forced me to be intentional.

If you've been making monthly payments through one of the income-based or extended plans, you may have no trouble making your minimum monthly student loan payment, but you also may not be making much progress. Refinancing can help you get focused and serious about paying off your loans.

Getting Paid

Did you know that you may actually be able to get paid for refinancing? No, this isn't some scam. This is just what companies are currently willing to do get you on board.

Refinance companies make money by the interest you pay them each month. Because pharmacists typically carry high debt loads in the six figures, refinance companies will make more money over the course of the loan versus those with much lower student loan balances.

Therefore, as an incentive for you to use a particular company, they will offer a cash bonus or welcome bonus.

Here's the best part!

You're not limited to doing this one time. With interest rates always changing, it's not uncommon for another company to provide a better rate than what you refinanced to the first time. You can refinance your loans multiple times and get cash bonuses from more than one company.

My wife and I actually made $2,700 in a single year doing this and were able to get a lower rate each time. It's worth noting that if you do this frequently, you may see a reduction in your credit score since every time a full application is submitted, there is a hard pull on your credit report.

YFP has partnered with multiple reputable student loan refinance companies that offer cash bonuses. Yes, YFP gets a referral bonus when you refinance through our link, but we have shifted the majority of the payout to you. You can go to www.yourfinancialpharmacist.com/refinance to check out the lenders we've partnered with and what cash bonuses they are currently offering.

Disadvantages of Refinancing

You may be thinking "Wow, I could be saving a ton if I refinance my student loans, but what's the catch?"

Refinancing is not without some drawbacks and it's important to know what you're giving up if you make the move.

First, once you refinance, you're automatically ineligible for any of the forgiveness programs. In addition, most private lenders do not offer income-driven plans, so you will lose the flexibility to change your monthly payments if you experience a sudden change in your income. Furthermore, the option to put your loans in deferment or forbearance will not likely be available.

Also, not all lenders will forgive your loans if you die or become permanently disabled. If you decide to go this route, you will want to know what their policy is on this. Regardless, you should have adequate life and disability insurance policies in place if these events were to occur.

If you want to compare rates with the top life and disability insurance companies, you can go to www.yourfinancialpharmacist.com/insurance-for-pharmacists.

Considerations When Refinancing

Choosing Which Loans to Refinance

If you have multiple student loans, you don't have to refinance all of them.

You can choose which loans you want to refinance. If some are already at a lower rate than what you can refinance to, you would obviously leave those alone.

Finding a Reputable Lender

Unfortunately, there are many scams and frauds out there. You want to have your guard up and make sure you are working with a reputable lender. Your Financial Pharmacist has partnered with several reputable lenders that you can feel confident with. You can also check out the Better Business Bureau to review ratings and reviews of prospective lenders.

Besides choosing a reputable lender, you want to be sure there is no origination fee for the service. There is a lot of competition in this refinance space, and companies are eager for your business. Most are willing to pay you to use their services. Bottom line, if there is any proposed charge to you, it's a major red flag.

Also, there should be no prepayment penalty. If you decide you want to pay off your loan faster than the term, you shouldn't incur any additional fees.

Types of Interest Rates

As mentioned, all federal loans have fixed interest rates, but that is not the case for refinanced loans.

Generally, like home mortgages, interest for refinanced student loans come in two flavors: fixed and variable. Fixed interest rates stay the same throughout the term and result in the same minimum monthly payment.

Variable interest rates tend to start out low, many times lower than fixed rates. However, variable interest rates can change depending on the Federal Reserve and LIBOR. There is usually a max or capped interest rate and a specific frequency in which it could change.

Although variable rates can be attractive, depending on the fluctuation, it could cost you thousands in interest if rates rise significantly during your payoff. If that has happened to you, then you want to try to refinance to a fixed rate as soon as possible.

Besides fixed and variable, you may also encounter hybrid interest rates. In general, these rates stay fixed for a certain number of years and then change to variable.

You'll want to consider the best type of interest rate for your needs.

Typical Requirements to Refinance

Private lenders will not refinance student loans for just anyone. You will be required to have a minimum credit score (usually at least 650), a minimum lending amount, proof of a certain level of income, and potentially a certain debt-to-income ratio. This will vary from lender to lender. Plus, these items will determine your eligibility *and* impact your quoted rate.

If for some reason you don't meet the minimum requirements, a prospective lender may ask for a co-signer. In general, that's not usually a good idea because it puts that person on the hook if you can't pay.

Getting Multiple Quotes

You have probably received mail or emails from companies encouraging you to refinance with them. Even though you may be familiar with some brands or have heard of good experiences about a particular one from friends and family, be sure you get multiple quotes to find the best deal.

Although we are not partners with all refinance companies, we have several you can check. To keep things organized, we have a spreadsheet that will help you collect and input all of your rates, which you can download at www.yourfinancialpharmacist.com/refitable.

When you are shopping around to find the best rate, companies will run a soft check of your credit to give you an accurate quote. This will not affect your credit score, but if you proceed to a full application, then you could see a very minor temporary drop.

The quotes you receive will usually be reported as fixed or variable along with the respective payment terms. Most companies have terms of 5, 7, 10, 15, and 20 years. Typically, the shorter the term, the better the rate.

In addition, keep in mind that your quoted rates are often shown with a built-in autopay discount.

They want to make sure they get their money!

Although there are many good companies that offer competitive rates, I do want to call one out specifically because it is unique.

First Republic Bank was founded in 1985 and offers general banking services. Their student loan refinance program really makes First Republic Bank stand out, as they offer extremely low interest rates and the opportunity to receive your interest money back. If you pay back the loan within four years, they will actually *give you back the interest you paid,* up to 2% of the original loan balance. This is exactly what happened with the loan my wife and I had with them. Because we paid it off fairly quickly, we got back over $1,500.

Similar to other lenders, they offer terms of 5, 7, 10, and 15 years. Instead of taking all of your financial information and then using an algorithm to give you a personalized interest rate, their rates are all or nothing. You either qualify or you don't.

You can learn more about First Republic and my personal experience using them by checking out this post at www.yourfinancialpharmacist .com/firstrepublicbank

Summary

The non-forgiveness payoff strategy offers the most flexibility when paying off your student loans. Although you'll choose a repayment plan with a specific term, you can always pay off the loans faster.

There are multiple options within the federal loan program and among private lenders. The federal loan program will give you greater protection as a borrower, but you can't change your interest rate, which is one of the limiting factors. Refinancing to a private lender can help you save a ton in interest, but you want to make sure you are choosing a reputable company and you understand your rights and responsibilities for the terms they offer.

Chapter 6

CHOOSING THE BEST STRATEGY

Hopefully by now you've realized that there are multiple strategies to take down your loans. More importantly, you recognize that there isn't one strategy that will work for everyone—but there *will* be one that works for you.

Let's walk through how to choose the best strategy for you.

Step 1: Check for all "free" money available

Before getting into the weeds and making things complicated with your student loans, the first thing you should do is to check for any and all free money that is available.

The availability of this strategy will depend not only on your employer but the accessibility of funds.

In Chapter 2, I discussed that the most generous programs for tuition reimbursement are through the federal government, such as the military, Veterans Affairs, and Indian Health Services. Beyond the availability of funds, your time of service will have a big impact on how much you are able to receive.

Therefore, if you still have not decided on where you're going to work or you're a new graduate and haven't already started working, the potential to take advantage of one of these programs could be a major determinant of your career decision or transition.

Remember there are also state-funded programs available for pharmacists. For these, as with federal programs, you may have to apply every year in order to continue to receive funds.

Step 2: Determine PSLF Eligibility

Once you've exhausted all tuition reimbursement options, you should analyze whether PSLF is an option.

PSLF is often the most beneficial strategy for pharmacists because it will result in the lowest monthly payment and the lowest total amount paid.

Remember, the easiest way to qualify for PSLF is to work for a government organization or a 501(c)(3) nonprofit, which includes many hospital systems.

Sure, there is a lot of concern and controversy with the logistical aspects and potential longevity of the program, but if you have done your due diligence to ensure you qualify and are meeting all the requirements, then you should feel confident about your decision.

Plus, you should feel a little relief knowing more and more borrowers are actually making it through the finish line.

I hear a lot of pharmacists in the YFP Facebook group say, "I wish I was eligible for PSLF."

And sometimes my response is, "Could you *become* eligible?"

Even if you've already made a career decision that landed you in a non-qualifying position, what about making a move to bring PSLF on the table?

I get that it could be tough to change employers if you are already established and are happy where you work. It could also take time and energy to find a qualifying position. But it's something to consider.

If PSLF is available and you are willing to go through all the hoops to meet the requirements, then there's no need to move on to step 3. Just keep good records and follow the recommendations to optimize your savings by lowering your AGI through tax-favored retirement contributions, as outlined in Chapter 3.

PSLF may not be the right strategy for you if you graduated with a much lower debt load than the typical pharmacist or you have a substantially higher income than the median pay. If this is the case, it's possible that nothing would be forgiven since the debt would be paid off earlier than 10 years, even with income-driven repayments.

Step 3: Assess Your Debt-to-Income Ratio

Things get interesting (not in the context of binging *The Pharmacist* on Netflix) if there aren't any tuition reimbursement programs available, if you don't qualify for PSLF, or if you can't switch to a position that qualifies for PSLF.

If this sounds like your situation, you may want to immediately consider refinancing options and call it a day.

However, remember there may be another option for you: Non-PSLF forgiveness.

You don't want to miss out on the potential benefits of the program if that strategy makes sense.

The biggest determinant of whether non-PSLF forgiveness is right for you will be your debt-to-income ratio. The higher that number, the more likely you are to benefit.

Usually, that is somewhere around 2:1 or greater.

If you recall, in order to have your loans forgiven outside of PSLF, you have to make income-driven payments for 20 to 25 years. This strategy only makes sense if, based on your debt-to-income ratio, your payments do not cover the bill over that timeframe. If they do, then there would be nothing to forgive at the end of the repayment term.

Step 4: Do the Math

The main determinant of your strategy at this point comes down to math.

You want to choose a strategy where you pay the least amount of money as legally possible, right?

Follow these steps to see how much you will pay over the course of the loan with different repayment strategies:

Enter your loan info in the loan simulator at www.studentaid.gov. Once logged in, you will be asked to provide your income, projected income growth, how you file your taxes, spousal loan and income, dependents, and contributions toward retirement accounts. Your loan information should already be populated, unless you didn't log in. Choose the "Pay the Lowest Total Amount Over Time" option.

If the simulator determines that there is a projected amount forgiven after 20 to 25 years on income-driven payments based on your debt-to-income ratio, estimate your tax bill based on the amount forgiven. While it's impossible to know exactly what your tax rate will be that far in the future, 25-35% is probably reasonable.

You will need to figure out how much to save each month to cover your tax bill. You can go to www.yourfinancialpharmacist.com/savings-goal-calculator and determine the monthly amount needed to reach that target based on years to save, how much you have already, and the expected annual rate of return.

This amount needs to be factored in with the total amount paid from the repayment estimator to get the actual cost of your loans over that time.

Obtain quotes from refinance companies to see what interest rates you have available based on the respective term. This will give you a more accurate comparison against non-PSLF forgiveness. You can fill out the YFP Refinance Comparison table at www.yourfinancialpharmacist.com/refitable, which will help you keep track of your rates. You can also check rates from other lenders and see how they compare.

If you don't have any income yet, you may not be able to get refinance offers. In that case, you can use our refinance calculator and put in assumptions about potential rates to obtain monthly payment amounts and to calculate the total amount paid. Remember to consider First Republic as an option if you live near a physical location and are able to meet their qualifications, as their rates are usually the lowest available.

Analyze and compare all of your repayment options. You will want to focus on the total amount paid and your estimated monthly payments. Remember to include the amount you need to save each month for the potential tax bomb as part of your overall monthly payment for Non-PSLF forgiveness.

Step 5: Evaluate Factors Beyond the Math

Beyond the math, there are some key questions that should be taken into consideration as they can impact your decision.

What can you afford?

You may have looked at your repayment options and found that refinancing to a five-year term will get you the lowest interest rate and result in paying the least compared to any other plan. However, if making that payment makes it difficult to eat every month, then it's really a moot point. Any option where you can't make the payment should be eliminated.

Even if you can "make" the payments, they could put a strain on your budget and compromise your ability to achieve your other goals, such as retirement and home buying.

That's why choosing the most aggressive term may not be realistic.

What is your attitude toward your student debt?

If you are someone who can't stand having debt, the thought of carrying it around for 20 to 25 years could be terrifying and you may rather pay it off faster, even if the math doesn't make sense. I know people who had the option of PSLF but decided to pay it off faster because they didn't want to hold on to their debt. You could say I was in that camp, but for me, it was more about not fully recognizing the benefits. It wasn't an informed decision; I want yours to be. And that depends on your own attitude and preferences.

If pursuing forgiveness, are you willing to accept the uncertainty of legislative changes?

As discussed, when it comes to forgiveness through PSLF or after 20 to 25 years with non-PSLF forgiveness, you are banking on the government following through. The negative publicity can be intimidating, and some people would rather take charge and make things happen on their own.

Choosing Your Strategy

Have you determined your strategy yet?

I know it's a big decision and the path you choose can impact many aspects of your life.

Figuring out the math behind your options is the best place to start because it takes all the emotions out of the equation.

The first number you should be focusing on is the total amount paid over the course of the loan.

Besides that, your monthly payment is important. Not only should you be able to afford your payments every month, they also can't be so large that you struggle to pay other monthly bills and fund other financial goals.

Since either of the forgiveness options are accomplished through one of the income-driven repayment plans, you shouldn't have much trouble making those payments.

This especially comes into play if you are going to pay back your loans outside of any forgiveness option, either through the federal loan program or a private lender. In the next chapter, I will discuss how to balance other financial priorities alongside making student loan payments.

Putting it All Together

Once you have determined your payoff strategy, you want to be as specific as possible on what that looks like.

If one of the forgiveness strategies is best for you, then refer to Chapters 3 and 4 to choose the optimal repayment plan.

You should be able to fill in the blanks to this statement:

The best student loan payoff strategy for me is _____ because _____. I will tackle my loans by choosing the _____ repayment plan.

Here are a few examples of what that could look like:

Example 1: The best student loan payoff strategy for me is the Public Service Loan Forgiveness program because it will result in the least amount paid over the life of the loan. I will accomplish this by choosing the Pay-as-You-Earn repayment plan.

Example 2: The best student loan payoff strategy for me is non-forgiveness via refinancing because it will result in the least amount paid over the life of the loan and allows me to be in control of when it is ultimately paid off. I will accomplish this by choosing a 10-year term with a fixed interest rate and make extra payments as often as I'm able to shorten the timeline. I will also consider refinancing multiple times if able to achieve a lower interest rate.

Example 3: The best student loan payoff strategy for me is non-forgiveness via the Federal Loan program because I'm not confident in my job stability and I want the protections in place. I will accomplish this by initially choosing the 10-year standard repayment plan.

Summary

Your strategy should be one that saves you the most money and also aligns with your goals.

You should first check for any free money available through tuition reimbursement programs. Then determine if you are eligible or could become eligible for PSLF. If not, then you should assess whether non-PSLF forgiveness makes sense based on your debt-to-income ratio. Otherwise, you are left with paying off loans through one of the repayment plans in the federal loan program or refinancing to a private lender and choosing a term.

Chapter 7

HOW TO MANAGE COMPETING FINANCIAL GOALS WITH STUDENT LOANS

Should I be doing X while paying off student loans?

This is one of the most commonly asked questions in personal finance.

Basically, insert any financial goal for "X": saving for retirement, buying a home, saving for a child's future tuition, buying a Tesla Model S Performance, etc.

You get the picture. Maybe you've had similar questions.

When people ask these kinds of questions, typically they are referring to whether they should pay more than the minimum payment on their student loans versus funding something else.

If you've gone down the internet rabbit hole to find the answer, you've probably realized there is no shortage of opinions on this topic from blogs, financial gurus, friends, and your cousin Larry.

So, who's right and what should YOU do?

Well, I'll just tell you the answer. You ready?

The answer is *it depends*.

I know. Very profound and insightful, right?

The problem is there are many factors that go into these kinds of decisions, making it difficult for blanket recommendations to stick.

What makes things even more difficult is present bias. By nature, we are impulsive and tend to make decisions that will make us feel good in the present instead of ones that promote some larger reward in the future. This is especially true when it comes to our finances. We spend on short-term pleasures such as eating out, going on vacations, or buying Kate Spade purses.

These are things above your essential expenses that compete for a chunk of your monthly budget, in addition to extra student loan payments and contributions toward other financial goals.

The bottom line is that w allocating your monthly disposable income is like many people's Facebook relationship statuses: "It's complicated."

However, a good place to start that will provide a little more clarity to that big financial question is to look through the lens of your specific student loan payoff strategy.

Factors Beyond Your Payoff Strategy

Before we look at each individual payoff strategy, I want to highlight some other factors you need to consider.

Disposable Income

Because your minimum monthly student loan payments will be dictated by the payoff strategy you choose, this will have a major impact on the amount of disposable income you have to allocate each month.

Disposable income is the amount of money you have to put toward financial goals each month. More specifically, it's your take-home pay minus essential and discretionary expenses. Think of essential expenses as housing, food, transportation, utilities, insurance premiums, and minimum payments on your debts. Discretionary items are nice to have, but in a true financial emergency, they can be cut.

The question is, how much disposable income *do* you have?

You can figure this out by having a rock-solid budget.

I know that budgeting is not very sexy, and some people would rather do longhand phenytoin pharmacokinetics. (Honestly, who wouldn't?)

However, having a budget and sticking to it is the best way to be intentional with your money, and it ultimately allows you to achieve your financial goals.

If you need some help fine-tuning or getting your budget set up, head on over to www.yourfinancialpharmacist.com/budget and grab our budgeting tool.

Knowing Your Financial Priorities

Even if you're a recent graduate, you may have already been bombarded by questions like "When are you going to buy a house?" or "Are you saving for retirement?"

You may have responded with an awkward smile or shrug, but in reality, you may be thinking "I'm just trying to get settled in my job and make my first student loan payment."

Figuring out your financial priorities can be difficult because they're usually determined by a combination of both math and emotions.

There are a lot of plans out there give step-by-step guidance on what you should do and when you should do it, but the problem is that these plans don't take into consideration the unique features of each student loan payoff strategy.

However, no matter what strategy you're in, I think there are three key priorities to focus on if you haven't done so already:

1. Pay off high-interest credit card debt

No one ever plans to go into credit card debt. It's often the result of either overspending or unexpected events or emergencies. Having credit card debt is a financial emergency in and of itself, however, given the typical ridiculously high interest rates.

If you're in this situation, you should make it a priority to get rid of it as soon as possible. You want to take advantage of compound interest and not have it work against you. This is priority number one.

2. Set up an emergency fund

If you've never had an unexpected car repair, medical expense, or other emergency, it's only a matter of time. Life happens and you better be prepared. Having a good chunk of cash on hand can mitigate emergencies that have the potential to derail your financial plan, including your student loans.

The textbook answer is to have three to six months of expenses saved in a liquid account that is easy to access. A good place to keep this is in a high-yield savings account or money market account. You can check some of the options we have reviewed at www.yourfinancialpharmacist.com/highyieldsavings

3. Contribute to get your full retirement match if available

While you may feel you can put off retirement savings for a few years, the reality is that you want to take advantage of compound interest, and the earlier you start contributing, the better.

Many companies offer a match program where they will put in a dollar amount equal to or a percentage of your contribution up to a max, such as 5%. This is essentially "free" money and, for most people, taking the match makes sense even while paying off student loans.

The main reason is because you can never recoup this benefit or "catch up" if you miss out on the opportunity.

Beyond these, it's important to have your financial priorities such as homebuying, saving, and other investing in place since they will ultimately determine how you will allocate your disposable income.

If you need help figuring them out, you can book a free call with one of our Certified Financial Planners™ at www.yourfinancialpharmacist.com/planning

Managing Financial Priorities Based on Payoff Strategy

Tuition Reimbursement

If you're going to get free money to go toward your student loans in exchange for putting in years of service, you want to figure out how to maximize that benefit.

Many programs provide you with money simply for time served. In other words, you don't need to prove the amount of money you paid toward your student loans in order to get the benefit. You just have to have loans.

This differs from programs such as the Education Debt Reduction Program offered through the Veterans Health Administration, where you get reimbursed for the payments you make. Currently, the maximum amount is $24,000 a year for five years, or a total of $120,000. In other words, if you pay $24,000 toward your loan in a year, you will be matched or reimbursed for that amount.

In this situation, your goal should be to figure out the least amount of money you have to pay out of pocket to get as much of the benefit as possible.

Although you may be tempted to accelerate your payoff, doing so could limit the total reimbursement amount. If one of these programs is offering enough to completely knock out your balance, instead of paying extra on your loans, consider looking to fund other financial goals such as retirement, buying a home, etc.

If by maximizing the total benefit, your entire student loan bill isn't covered, then making additional or extra payments to speed up your payoff could make sense.

You can refer to chapter 2 for available federal tuition reimbursement programs.

PSLF

If you are all in on PSLF, do not make extra student loan payments. I repeat, do *not* make extra student loan payments.

First, doing so will not speed up the process. You can only make a single payment in a month to count toward PSLF, and you have to do that 120 times.

Second, if you make extra student loan payments, it's possible you could reduce the loan balance to the point where there's nothing to forgive after 10 years. Your goal is to pay the least amount of money over 10 years, since any remaining balance is forgiven tax-free.

In addition, remember that you actually get rewarded for saving money for retirement while pursuing PSLF. Since your monthly payments are determined by your adjusted gross income, making traditional 401(k) contributions and/or Health Savings Account contributions will lower that amount and thereby lower your overall total bill.

The bottom line is this: figure out the least amount of money you have to legally pay every month and then fund your remaining financial priorities.

Non–PSLF Forgiveness

Similar to PSLF, with non-PSLF forgiveness you are going to make income-driven payments except they are going to be for 20 to 25 years depending on the repayment plan you're in.

Again, you want to pay the least amount over time, so making payments beyond your minimum doesn't make a whole lot of sense, especially if it's to the point where nothing is even forgiven after 20 to 25 years.

The only advantage of doing that would be to lower your amount forgiven and subsequently your tax bill. However, in that case, you may be better off just refinancing.

In addition, remember that if you have 20 to 25 years to save for that tax bill, and, assuming you get a decent rate of return over that time, you only need to actively save a fraction of the projected amount as discussed in Chapter 4.

Therefore, similar to PSLF, aim to pay the least amount in payments over time. You can do this in part by maximizing traditional 401k contributions. In addition, make sure you are saving enough each month to cover the future tax bill. You can get an estimate by going to www.yourfinancialpharmacist.com/savings-goal-calculator.

Beyond that, fund your other priorities.

Non-Forgiveness

Now to get down to business. This chapter is really focused on those who are pursuing the non-forgiveness strategy. Because there is no set timeline for loan payoff and you have the most flexibility, it can be difficult to determine which financial priorities to focus on.

The question now becomes this: "If I'm not eligible for forgiveness or tuition reimbursement programs, how fast should I pay off my student loans and should I be contributing to other financial goals along the way?"

Sometimes people think about this as an all or none situation. You either go all in and throw every extra dollar you can to pay off your loans as fast as possible or you can extend the term as long as possible, make the minimum payments, and any extra money goes toward retirement, buying a home, purchasing an investment property, etc.

The reality is that there are many repayment timelines, from 0 to 30 years, and you need to figure out where you want to fall on that. Here's what I mean: If for some strange reason you had the money today in cash to pay off your loans, you could make it happen. Or, through a Direct Consolidation loan, you can extend payments up to 30 years. And there's a spectrum between the two extremes.

Most pharmacists end up almost exactly in the middle of that spectrum. In a study by Credible, pharmacists took an average of 14.5 years to pay off their student loans.

Surprised?

You probably know people who made it happen much faster and those who extended their payoff beyond that.

The bigger your monthly payments, the faster your loans will be paid off and the less interest will be paid over the course of the loan. But it also limits your ability to contribute toward other financial goals simultaneously.

While again, no one answer is going to work for everyone, I think there are some key factors to consider that may help determine how far to the left or right of the scale you want to move.

Working Years Remaining

Not every pharmacist graduates with a PharmD at the traditional age of their mid-twenties. In fact, about half of my class were in their late thirties and this was a second career for them. Shoutout to the first graduating class of NEOMED!

While not a blanket statement, those graduating and starting their pharmacy career at a later stage in life are likely going to have fewer working years than traditional graduates.

Why is that important?

If you have fewer total working years ahead, that means you have a shorter time frame for compound interest to work. If you're someone in this situation, focusing solely on paying off your student loans could significantly stunt your retirement nest egg.

In addition, remember that although the IRS authorizes catch-up contributions for retirement accounts for those age 50 and older, those are less than what the annual contributions are.

In other words, once you've missed out for the year maxing out a 401(k) or HSA, you can never fully "catch up."

Interest Rate of Student Loans and Time in Debt

Although federal interest rates are generally in the 6 to 8% range, what if you were able to get your rate down ultra-low, to 2 to 3%? Would you still pay off your loans aggressively?

A great argument that often comes up is: "If I can make a 7% rate of return in the stock market, why would I pay extra on loans that are 3% interest?"

Based on historical returns, it's a fair assumption that you *could* get a return around 7%, but over how many years? Often times, when people make these kinds of statements, they forget that typically these are market returns over at least a 10-year period.

A lot can happen in the market in a short period of time, so generally, this statement is more likely to be true if you anticipate your loan payoff taking 10 years or more.

Now what about the other scenario, where your student loan interest rates are high? While you can refinance, what if for some reason your credit score or other factors prevent you from being able to? Or what if market rates are high and they won't improve your situation much?

In that case, you may want to be more aggressive with your payments and shorten your time to pay them off.

Another consideration is that if you can knock out your loans relatively quickly, such as in one to two years, you're not giving up much time in the stock market or the ability to fund other goals.

Emotional Feelings about Loans

While math and interest rates are important, what about how you feel about being in debt and having student loans?

Student loan debt is one of the biggest stressors among young adults. In a study performed by the University of South Carolina on 25- to 31-year-olds, it was concluded that there was a positive correlation between the amount of student loan debt and depressive symptoms. In other words, the higher the debt load, the more depressed the subject was.

No surprises there, right?

According to Student Loan Hero, people can lose sleep over their student loans or feel physical symptoms like headaches and muscle tension due to stress stemming from their debt. Student loans and other debt also can cause people to isolate themselves, putting a strain on relationships with family and friends.

This emotional stress and poor sense of well-being can be a major motivator to get rid of your loans ASAP. It definitely was for me. And I'll give you a perfect example where I followed my emotions over math.

In my wife's and my final 14 months of having student loans, we were able to refinance to a 1.95% fixed interest rate. Although the term was for five years, we decided to knock it out a lot faster.

I know that I could have beat 0% in almost any other investment. But the feeling of becoming debt-free was more important and having more disposable income every month after the final student loan payment was a relief.

Because there's such an emotional impact with student loans, this has to factor into your equation when determining your payoff timeline. However, it's important to keep the math front and center so that your emotions don't completely override good financial sense.

Putting it Together

Where do you fall on the payoff timeline?

Are you going to slow-pay your student loans and focus on other goals, pay them off ASAP, or are you somewhere in between?

Regardless of what your plan is, make sure you are as specific as possible and have clarity on how you are going to make it happen.

In the last chapter, I had you fill in the blanks for your payoff strategy and the subsequent repayment plan to make it happen.

If your strategy is non-forgiveness, hopefully this chapter helped you to structure that plan.

As an example, I want to share what our plan was:

The best student loan strategy for us is non-forgiveness via refinancing our federal loans because it will result in the least amount paid over the life of the loan and allows us to be in control of when it is ultimately paid off.

We will accomplish this by choosing a five-year fixed term because we are able to get the lowest interest rate available. We will also consider refinancing multiple times if we're able to achieve a lower interest rate.

During our payoff, we will also contribute enough money to obtain the full retirement match offered by our employers and fully fund a Health Savings Account every year.

Any disposable income, windfall money, bonuses, or other unexpected income will go toward paying extra on the student loans to accelerate the payoff.

Your plan could be something similar or it could include other financial goals, such as simultaneously saving for a home or funding kids' college. Regardless, the key is being specific and having a plan.

Considerations for Accelerating Your Payoff

Since there are many pharmacists who paid off their loans in record time and many who want to make that happen, I had to include a section on this.

I was in this camp, too!

You've probably heard of people doing some crazy things to knock out their loans faster, like moving into a tiny home, living in a van down by the river, growing their own food, and making bicycles their primary means of transportation.

You don't have to get that extreme, but you could.

To accelerate your payoff, it really comes down to making bigger or extra payments.

But, how?

You can either reduce monthly expenses, make more money, or both. These will have the biggest impact on your timeline.

If you want some ideas on how to do that, consider checking out the posts www.yourfinancialpharmacist.com/how-to-save-half-of-your-income and www.yourfinancialpharmacist.com/14 for some ways to grow your monthly income.

Another move that I talked about already is refinancing, and potentially doing so multiple times. If you make the same monthly payment with a lower interest rate as you did when the rate was higher, a greater percentage of the payment will go toward the principal, thereby cutting down your payoff timeline.

Lastly, and one of my favorite methods to help knock out student loans, is to take advantage of windfall money.

This isn't money that you serendipitously find outside on the ground while going for an evening stroll—although that's always nice, too.

I'm talking about unexpected income that comes your way. Some of the common ones include bonuses from work, profit shares from a business, gift money from a friend or relative, an inheritance, a refund from your taxes, and gambling winnings (although this is not something I am necessarily promoting).

One of these came our way when we were in the middle of our payoff. My wife's parents had been paying the premiums on a cash value permanent life insurance policy since she was born, and it had around $10,000 in it.

Because we had plenty of term life insurance coverage, they ended up cashing out the policy and gifted us the money.

Throwing that big of a chunk at the debt felt awesome!

Some people treat windfall money differently than they would treat ordinary income. This has been described as a behavioral bias known as mental accounting.

You know what I'm talking about, right?

"Oh, that's birthday money so I can spend it on clothes," as my wife would often say.

Having your financial goals and priorities in place will be key as you should have a plan for exactly what you will do with windfall money.

To see the impact of making extra monthly payments or a lump sum payment on your student payoff timeline, you can go to www.yourfinancial-pharmacist.com/early-payoff-calculator

Summary

You are going to have one or more competing financial priorities as you pay off student loans. These include funding retirement accounts and other investments, saving for a home purchase, and funding kids' tuition, in addition to just living life.

While some advocate for paying off your student loans as fast as possible while ignoring all other goals, that may not always be the best move, as there is an opportunity cost for doing so.

That's why funding multiple goals simultaneously can also be a good move. You should carefully consider all the factors and establish a solid, specific goal for your own payoff strategy.

Chapter 8

HOW TO MANAGE STUDENT LOANS AS A FELLOW OR RESIDENT

Just about halfway through my residency, I got *the letter*. Well, actually I got two.

You know the one I'm talking about, right?

That dreaded first student loan payment notice.

The grace period had ended and it was time to start making payments as indicated several years ago on my promissory notes.

Two loan servicers meant I would be making two different payments each month starting from that point. I'll fully admit that I had no idea what I was doing and since there was no way I could make the 10-year standard payments under the federal loan program, I just changed them to the 25-year extended plan.

That seemed like a good move for the time being to give me some breathing room so I could still pay my other bills and have a little money for fun.

But after about two months of doing that, I realized *even that* was a stretch. Because my balance was about $200,000, the payments on the extended plan were still about half of my income!

I decided to put one of the chunks of my loans in forbearance. That gave my budget a little more cushion for the next six months and I, again, thought that was a good move at the time.

But I had messed up. In reality, there were much better options.

What do I do right now?

If you recently graduated and you're in a residency program or fellowship, you may be thinking, "All of this information is great about finding my strategy, but I'm not making the typical pharmacist salary yet, so what can I do right now?"

When you're making about a third of what most pharmacists make, it can be overwhelming trying to face your loans. That's why your main goal should be to survive!

You have to be able to make monthly payments that still allow you to pay rent, get groceries, and maybe have a little fun.

But you have to be strategic on how you do that.

Assuming most of your loans are federal and you are about to go into repayment for the first time, one of the best initial moves is to do a Direct Consolidation Loan.

This will combine all your federal loans into one with a weighted interest rate which will be serviced by a single lender. Not only will this make things simpler, but it will also automatically convert and make essentially all loans eligible for one of the income-driven repayment plans that qualify for PSLF or non-PSLF forgiveness.

If you have a typical pharmacy student loan balance and no other income sources, it is likely going to be difficult to afford any of the monthly payments aside from the income-driven plans.

Of course, you could claim forbearance to temporarily stop making payments in the name of financial hardship like I did, but here's the issue: Interest will accrue daily when your loans are in that status and you cannot make any qualifying payments toward either forgiveness program.

Refinancing will pretty much be off the table, since most companies probably won't approve you based on your debt-to-income ratio.

Besides that, the furthest you can stretch your loan is usually 20 years. And even on a 20-year term, with a typical debt load, that will still be a huge payment to make as a resident.

Choosing the Best Income-Driven Repayment Plan

One of the biggest benefits of making payments through the income-driven plans is that they are based on your previous year's earnings from your tax return. That's good news if you're a resident or fellow or if you didn't make much money as a student.

Therefore, your monthly payments could literally be $0. Zero-dollar payments still count as "qualifying payments," too, whether it's for PSLF or non-PSLF forgiveness.

The income-driven repayment plan you choose will depend on what your anticipated overall strategy will be.

Anticipated Strategy: Non-forgiveness

If you're planning to eventually work at a for-profit company such as a community pharmacy and you may eventually refinance, REPAYE can be a good option.

Under REPAYE, for all Direct Unsubsidized loans, the government will pay 50% of the interest that accrues every month if your loan payment is less than the amount of the monthly interest.

Let's assume you have $160,000 in student loans at 7% interest. $933 in interest will accrue every month as soon as the grace period ends. If your payment is $0, which would be the case if you had no income last year, the amount of interest that would accrue would only be $466.

This will allow you to finish your training with the lowest loan balance possible as you transition to a higher salary.

If your budget allows and you do have some disposable income, then you could technically make additional payments beyond what's set as your minimum.

However, this won't make sense if there's a chance forgiveness will be an option after your residency or fellowship.

Anticipated Strategy: Non–PSLF forgiveness

If you don't think you will be working for a qualifying PSLF employer and you will have a large debt-to-income ratio (such as 2:1 or more), PAYE would be a good option.

With PAYE or IBR-New, you can get forgiveness after 20 years or 240 qualifying income-driven repayments. With either of these plans, you also get the option to file your taxes separately if married, which could be beneficial. And you will never pay more than the payment for the standard 10-year plan.

Anticipated Strategy: PSLF forgiveness

If you anticipate working for the government or a non-profit organization eligible for PSLF, PAYE or REPAYE will be good options. A key consideration for PAYE is that spousal income comes into play depending on how your taxes are filed, as discussed in chapter 3.

Remember, PSLF is often the most beneficial payoff strategy because it will often result in the lowest amount paid over the life of your loans. Therefore, when you are evaluating employment options post-residency or fellowship, you definitely want to consider qualifying employers, as this is a huge potential benefit.

Summary

Making student loan payments during residency or fellowship can be difficult, given that most pharmacists in these training programs make about one-third the typical pharmacist salary.

Regardless of what your overall anticipated student loan strategy will be, doing a Direct Consolidation Loan and choosing an income-driven repayment plan will be the best option for most pharmacists who are starting repayment for the first time.

This will allow you to make $0 or low monthly payments, which is key to financially surviving your residency. In addition, these low payments will be considered qualifying payments if you're pursuing PSLF or non-PSL forgiveness.

If a forgiveness plan is not likely going to be pursued, then REPAYE is a good option because of the interest subsidy, which helps control the growth of the loan balance.

Chapter 9

HOW TO HANDLE STUDENT LOANS DURING A JOB LOSS OR FINANCIAL HARDSHIP

In October 2019, the California Board of Pharmacy invalidated around 1,400 exam results for California Practice Standards and Jurisprudence Examination for Pharmacists (CPJE) because of a cheating scandal. Somehow there was a leak of over 100 questions that pharmacists could have had access to prior to taking the exam.

This caused a significant delay in thousands of pharmacists being able to become fully licensed and practice in the state of California, and subsequently temporarily without a job or an income.

At that time, the grace period for federal loans was ending soon for most. As a result, one of the biggest questions that came up was, "What do I do about starting repayment?"

Although this is one of the more unusual situations pharmacists have faced when it comes to being able to repay loans, financial hardships do happen and it can make your student loans feel even more overwhelming than they already are.

With a number of brick-and-mortar community pharmacies closing and downsizing, many pharmacists are left between jobs and in a difficult transition period.

Some pharmacists are still looking for their first job after graduation or post-graduate programs.

Others are knee-deep in credit card debt, mortgage payments, and other financial obligations, making it difficult to pay their monthly student loan bill.

If you're unfortunately in one of these positions, let's take a look at what your options are. These are primarily dictated by the type of student loans you have.

Federal Loans

One of the greatest benefits of the federal loan program is that you have a lot of rights and safeguards available. These can help prevent you from defaulting on your loans, getting sued, or even having your wages garnished.

Keep in mind, some states are preventing pharmacists and other medical professionals from being licensed or renewing their licenses if their loans are in default, so this is a big deal.

Under the federal loan program, you have the right to prepay your loans without penalty. You have the right to a grace period. But you also have the right to request deferment or forbearance and change your repayment plan at any time.

That's good news because these are methods to help you through a tough time.

Deferment and forbearance are similar in that they are a means for you to temporarily stop making student loan payments.

The biggest difference between the two is that in deferment, interest will not accrue on subsidized federal loans, whereas in forbearance, all federal loans will accrue interest.

There are also more specific eligibility criteria for deferment. These include economic hardship or unemployment, pursuing a graduate fellowship, being enrolled at least half-time at an eligible college, being in active military service, or in a rehabilitation program for drug or alcohol abuse or mental health.

For forbearance, you can request on the grounds of financial hardship, medical expenses, or change in employment.

While these may seem like reasonable options, I would strongly urge you to consider them as a last resort. That's because switching your repayment plan to an income-driven one is usually a better move.

With the income-driven plans, you can report your income to the Department of Education, especially if it has decreased since your last tax filing.

If you're in the worst-case scenario where you have zero income, you can still make $0 payments, and you would not have to report a change in income until you re-certify the following year.

The good news is that $0 payments still count as "qualifying payments" whether it's for PSLF or non-PSLF forgiveness, although they technically will not count for PSLF until you have started employment with a qualifying employer.

If you're about to enter repayment, you should apply for the Direct Consolidation Loan. This will convert all your selected federal loans into one and will unlock the income-driven repayment plans that are eligible for PSLF and non-PSLF forgiveness.

The optimal repayment plan will depend on a few things. If you're planning to work at a for-profit company such as a community pharmacy and may eventually refinance, REPAYE can be a good option, as outlined in the previous chapter, given that the government will pay 50% of the interest that accrues every month if your loan payment is less than the monthly interest. This can control the growth of the loan during this period and then, once your income is stable, you can be much more aggressive with your payoff if that's your goal.

If you anticipate that your annual income will be half or less than half of your student loan balance, PAYE would be a good option because you can get forgiveness after making qualifying payments for 20 years.

Private Loans

The moves I just talked about are only going to work if you have federal loans.

If for some reason you have private loans or you have already refinanced your loans, you, unfortunately, won't have the same safeguards and options available in the federal loan program.

Therefore, you will have to work with your individual lender to find out what you can do. Some private lenders offer income-based payment options, interest-only payments, or some form of forbearance.

Another potential option is to extend the loan as far out as possible (such as 20 years) to get the lowest monthly payment possible.

How this affects your payoff strategy

In the previous chapters, I talked a lot about crafting your student loan payoff strategy. Obviously, financial hardship can temporarily derail your plan and force you to hit pause.

In many cases, once your income is stable again, you can simply continue the plan you already developed, assuming most of the variables haven't changed.

However, you may also have to re-evaluate your situation and go through the process of determining the best payoff strategy for you based on what's happening now.

Many people have had to change course because of unfortunate circumstances and that's OK. The key is being intentional about your plan.

Summary

Financial hardships can greatly affect your ability to make student loan payments. The federal loan program has many options to assist you during a tough time. Although deferment or forbearance are options, most of the time, choosing an income-driven plan will be a better option.

Options to deal with financial crises when you have private loans will be dependent on the individual lender.

Hopefully, your financial hardship is temporary. Once your income is stable again, you can resume your original student loan payoff strategy. However, you may also have to scrap your original plan and create a new one if your situation has significantly changed. The key is having a specific plan, even if you have to update or change it based on your circumstances. Your plan should always seek to meet your needs in the most effective, low-cost way possible.

If you need some help finding a position or transitioning to another pharmacy career, I recommend checking out TheHappyPharmD.com. Alex Barker, PharmD, created a platform around helping pharmacists find inspiring work and lives, primarily by assisting them in transitioning to pharmacy and non-pharmacy jobs they are passionate about.

CONCLUSION

Looking back, I had a really hard time at first coming to terms with having a combined student loan debt of $400,000.

It definitely wasn't easy starting off a marriage that way.

Personally, I had a lot of anxiety about it and even would have difficulty getting to sleep over it some nights.

That was until I had a plan and got confident about it. Even though it wasn't *the best* plan.

I made a bunch of mistakes along the way, which made me pay more than I needed to. But that doesn't have to be your story.

Whether you're facing $50,000 or $400,000 in student loan debt, the bottom line is you have options.

Having clarity about your plan can take an immense weight off your shoulders, allowing you to focus on other financial goals and live your life.

I know firsthand how difficult and overwhelming it can be looking six figures of debt right in the face and trying to figure out what to do.

Be intentional. Develop a plan. Execute and adapt as necessary.

And then enjoy the security and financial freedom of paying off those loans!

ADDITIONAL RESOURCES

1-on-1 Consults

Since every pharmacist's student loan situation is unique, it's possible your specific questions may not have been answered. In that case, I recommend you reach out to our financial planning team at www.yourfinancialpharmacist.com/planning.

We have helped many pharmacists, even with really high debt loads, navigate the PSLF program, prepare for taxable forgiveness, determine how to file taxes when married, and figure out if refinancing makes sense.

Calculators

Several calculators were mentioned throughout the book and most can be found at www.yourfinancialpharmacist.com. To find out your estimated forgiveness, income-driven payments, and potential tax obligations, you can go to www.studentaid.gov.

Tuition Reimbursement/Repayment Programs

For a complete list of the most up-to-date national and state tuition repayment programs, you can go to www.pharmdloans.com/#bonus

Student Loan Refinancing

As mentioned in the book, Your Financial Pharmacist has partnered with several student loan refinance companies to help you find the lowest rate and term that works for you. In addition, you can get a cashback bonus of

$800 or more depending on which company you use. You can learn more at yourfinanciapharmacist.com/refinance.

Your Financial Pharmacist Podcast

If you're a pharmacist, resident, or student looking for weekly financial tips with your student loans, investing, home buying, or other topics, you should definitely check out our podcast. We also talk about unique careers and side hustles to give you ideas on how to make more money.

Available on all the major podcast platforms.

Share Your Victories

One of the most powerful ways to stay motivated and help others on their student loan journey is to share your experience. And one of the best ways to do this is through our Facebook group, which has more than 5,000 pharmacists helping each other get confident with their money and take down their loans. You can join the conversation at yourfinancialpharmacist.com/facebook.

ACKNOWLEDGMENTS

Caitlin Boyle, Director of Content Management at Your Financial Pharmacist, for collecting, organizing, and proofreading all of the content within the book.

Tim Baker, CFP® and Director of Financial Planning at Your Financial Pharmacist, for providing an expert review of the content.

Tim Ulbrich, PharmD, co-founder and CEO of Your Financial Pharmacist, for writing the Foreword.

Justin Greer, Emily Chambers, Rochelle Deans, Azul Terronez, and the team at *Authors Who Lead* for providing copyediting and interior design services.

Arbëresh Dalipi for the cover design.

ABOUT THE AUTHOR

Tim Church, PharmD, CDE

Tim is the Director of Getting Things Done at Your Financial Pharmacist and a clinical pharmacy specialist at the West Palm Beach VA Medical Center.

He is also the author of *Seven Figure Pharmacist: How to Maximize Your Income, Eliminate Debt, and Create Wealth* and *When Eating Right Isn't Enough: The Top 5 Medications to Control Your Type 2 Diabetes.*

Tim lives in Palm Beach Gardens, FL with his wife, Andria.